Your Money
个人理财

（英）格里·贝利 费利西娅·劳◎著
（英）马克·比奇◎插图
傅瑞蓉◎译

目录 Contents

4～5　钱是什么？
钱就是你口袋或钱包里的东西吗？或者还包括其他更多的东西？

6～7　钱是一种必不可少的东西
有了钱，你就可以做很多事情。你要让钱流动起来。

8～9　钱没有脚，却可以到处走动
你买东西付了钱，但是钱是不会停下来不动的。

10～17　收到钱
这是大好事，你有自己的钱了。

18～19　当你有钱时的三种选择
你可以花掉它、存起来或捐给别人。

20～27　存起来
存钱的最好办法是把它交给别人，让别人去把它变得越来越多。

28～37　花掉它
把钱用在刀刃上，不要浪费宝贵的现金。

38～39　真是浪费
轻信他人会导致你把钱花在购买不需要的东西上。

40～43　借钱与债务
即使你是从朋友或家人手中借的钱，负债也可能会使你陷入麻烦之中。

44～45　做好预算
做好预算，这样管好你的钱就容易多了。

46～47 **统计结果如何？**
　　　　统计数据告诉我们，你有多少钱，你是怎么花钱的。

48～51 **把钱捐给别人**
　　　　捐出一点钱，你就能帮助世界各地有需要的人。

52～53 **富裕与贫穷**
　　　　财富真的能带来幸福吗？或者它反而会令你沮丧？

54～55 **虚拟货币**
　　　　这种你看不见摸不着的钱是真正的钱吗？

56～57 **未来……**
　　　　未来会怎样？

58～59 **讨论**
　　　　钱不会从树上长出来，我们要学会挣钱、花钱、节
　　　　约钱和做好开支预算。

60～61 **中英文术语对照表**

62～63 **索引**

　　64 **译后记**

　　　　附　英文影印版

钱是什么？

钱是什么？对于这个问题，答案似乎是显而易见的，钱就是躺在你口袋里或钱包里的、会发出叮叮当当响声的那个东西。当然，钞票也是钱，它来得快去得也快。但是，如果这些硬币和纸币是来自另外一个国家的，并且它们在你自己的国家连一张公交车票都无法买到，这时你还能称它们为钱吗？对于那些塑料做的钱，即借记卡和信用卡，你又是怎么看的呢？

钱是一种承诺

当然，你最好随时随地都带着一些硬币和纸币，尤其这些纸币或许只不过是一小张一小张的纸，但是它们具有钱的功能，它们是目前最流行的钱的形式。然后就是信用卡和黄金，它们也是钱，对吗？甚至还有一种钱，你看不见，摸不着，它就是电子货币。那么，这些都是真正的钱吗？

钱会不会过时呀……

因此，显而易见，钱的形态和形式一直都在发生着变化，虽然它的变化并不总是像从玛瑙、贝壳变为借记卡那么引人注目。此外，在各种场合和各个地方，人们使用钱的方式也并非都是一成不变的。这主要是因为钱并不仅仅关乎现金——纸币和硬币，也并不仅仅关乎信用卡，它还关乎银行和储蓄。

钱已经有6 000年的历史了

当我们弄清楚，什么可以被当做钱、什么不能被当做钱时，我们就会发现，在过去各种各样的、令人意想不到的东西，都曾经被我们当钱来使用过，比如琥珀、珠子、玛瑙、贝壳、鼓、蛋、羽毛等。

实际上，几乎任何东西都可以被当做钱来使用，甚至可以是几只羊，只要人们都认可它们的价值就行了。

钱以各种形式存在已经有6 000年的时间了。事实上，钱并不只是出现在某一个地方，它形式多样，在世界上各个不同的地方都曾出现过。

但是无论拿什么来当钱，它总是具备以下四个特征：

* 每个人都同意使用它。
* 每个人都同意它可以以不同的方式被使用。
* 每个人都一致同意它有价值，而且可以对它做出更改，但这种更改必须是大家都能接受的。
* 每个人都同意尊重它所代表的东西。

因此，让我们来搞清楚钱是如何为你工作的吧！

钱是一种必不可少的东西

你有钱吗？今天你让你口袋里的钱发出叮叮当当的响声了吗？你的手提袋里有一个装满硬币和纸币的钱包吗？或者，你是不是拥有一个储钱罐，那里塞满了你的零花钱？又或者你已经拥有自己的储蓄或银行账号了吗？

你有钱

如果你的情况符合上面所列举的任何一条，那么，你就是一个有钱的人了，而且随着时间的推移，日积月累，你的钱可能会越来越多。

钱会进进出出

钱就像是水，它会自由地流动，在每个人的口袋里进进出出。在你的一生中，它肯定会从你的口袋里流进流出，但是它流出去的速度会比流进来的速度更快吗？

如果钱流进了你的口袋，那么，这就是你的收入了。这可能是你的工作所得，也可能是别人给你的零花钱，还有可能是你得到的礼物，或者可能是别人送给你的。如果钱流出了你的口袋，那么，这就是你的支出了，你可能拿钱买东西了。如果钱流进你口袋的速度超过了流出你口袋的速度，那么，你就会变得富有起来；如果相反，你就可能有麻烦了。

钱也是一种非常有趣的东西

赚钱是一件乐事,当然花钱也是一件乐事。不过事实上你可以做得比这更好。你可以让你的钱再生钱,或者把你的钱投资出去。这是一个真正的挑战!

你可以用一种特殊的方式把它花掉,这样你在赚钱的同时又在花钱了。这是一个更大的挑战!

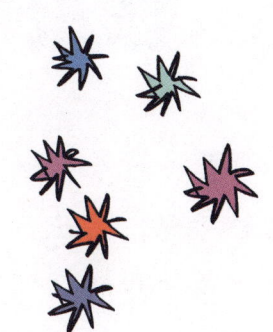

或者你可以与他人分享,你可以充分利用你的钱去帮助那些真正需要帮助的人。你可以想象一下接受你帮助的那个人。

* 我们常常会想到钱并谈论钱。
* 我们喜欢有钱,没有钱我们什么也买不到。
* 我们需要用它来购买一些如食物和住房之类的生活必需品。
* 钱可以买到一些有趣的东西,我们因此而得到某种享受。

因此,钱是一种必不可少的东西。你离不开钱,不过这并不是一件坏事;正好相反,钱是好东西,你可以随心所欲地使用它,它会给你带来乐趣。钱会生钱,你也可以开心地花钱,你更可以拿它来帮助别人。

越早开始越好!

钱没有脚，却可以到处走动

1 你想要购买一些口香糖，因此你拿出几枚硬币放到商店的柜台上，收银员收下了它们。

6 这些硬币最后流通到了一个孩子的手中。半个小时后，这些硬币又被递交到了当地糖果店的收银台上。

你在花钱时，钱就进入了流通领域并开始流通了

购买东西时，你会把钱付给店主，而店主会把钱存入银行，银行又会把钱转交给别人……

2 收银台里的钱不断地进进出出。

3 这些硬币发现自己在同一天里进出了四个不同的收银台。

5 它们仅仅在银行里待了两天，然后就又被一个兑换零钱的娱乐商场的老板兑换走了。

4 在周末时，它们被装进了袋子，并被交给了银行。

事实

* 在货币的流通过程中，年轻人所起的作用是让钱越来越多，这其中也包括你。

* 你不仅仅是一个购买者或者一个消费者，你还是货币循环过程中的重要组成部分。

* 年轻人不会拥有过多的钱，消费也不是他们需要做的唯一的一件事情。现在该是他们学习理财的时候了。

* 年轻人的工作会经常发生变动。社会上稳定的工作并不多，但是创业的机会却很多。你需要让自己变得更强大，你需要获得更多的帮助，你也需要有责任心。

* 你是一个年轻人，你可能缺乏经验，但是你可以把你所拥有的以下这些无价的资产拿出来与他人竞争：彬彬有礼、守时、聪明睿智、有责任心、讲诚信，人们会因为你所拥有的这些品质而投资于你。

美好的未来正在向你招手……你可能会拥有更多的钱，甚至可能会远远超过你的父母。会有更多的机会到你面前来！

收到钱

当你意外地得到一笔钱时，那种感觉真是太棒了。当你从小水沟里或者从垃圾堆的一个鞋盒里发现一枚硬币时，你可能会小小地激动一下。但可恨的是，你总是碰不到这样的好事。不过没关系的（惊喜！惊喜！），就是现在，请你马上行动起来，以你自己的名义存下一笔钱，或者在将来的某个时候你意外地得到了一笔钱，这两件事都有可能会改变你的生活。

生日时收到的钱

当你的生日来临时，你可能会收到那些疼爱你的亲戚朋友送给你的钱。或许，你刚出生时就已经收到过钱了。在这种情况下，你的父母可能已经以你的名义为你开设了一个银行账号或者储蓄账号了，并且还很有可能，这么多年来，你的父母一直在不断地往那个账号里存钱，只不过他们忘记告诉你罢了。是不是这样？

信托基金

你的父母甚至可能已经为你建立了一个信托基金。有时候,大人们会在银行里设立信托基金,或者把钱放在贷款或储蓄账户里进行投资,直到有一天孩子们长大了能够自己使用这笔资金为止。对于这种信托基金,人们通常会设立一个年限,在此之前无法动用它。

继承得到的钱

当某人的某个亲人去世时,他从死去的亲人那里获得了一笔钱,这就是继承所得。不过这种获得钱的方式是令人悲伤的。遗嘱是一份法律文件,在遗嘱中会明确规定当一个人去世后,该如何处理他的财产。如果没有遗嘱,那么,死者就会被称为无遗嘱死亡者。在这种情况下,到底由谁来继承死者的遗产,将由法律来决定。某人可能会成为继承者,不过是由一个陌生执法者来决定他能够得到多少。

你的财产

如果这些意外之财落到了你的头上,自不必说,你应该把它们用到刀刃上。如果你有了储蓄债券,或者信托基金,或者银行账户,或者其他任何形式的钱,那么,就可以说你拥有了自己的资产。资产是指你的财务价值,它被称为净值。随着你年龄的增加,净资产对你会越来越重要,它能够让你得到银行的财务支持以实现你的梦想,它能够帮助你读完大学,也能资助你进行环球游学。

零花钱

零花钱是一种固定收入

零花钱是你所获得的固定收入的第一站。基本上你每个星期都能准时而全额地获得一小笔零花钱。零花钱的来源通常很稳定,你完全可以依赖它。也就是说,在零花钱还没有到手之前,你就可以好好地计划着怎么花这笔钱了。

你是喜欢零花钱以周津贴的方式还是以月津贴的方式给你,这取决于你的家庭预算安排,当然它也同样取决于你的财务计划,即你相信自己这些零花钱能维持多久。财务计划就是人们所称的"预算"。如果你觉得你第一个星期就可能会把零花钱花光,那么采取月津贴的方式就不合适了!

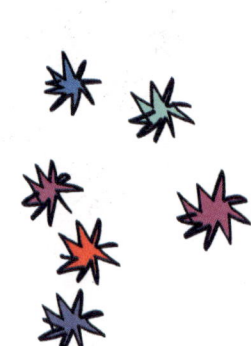

你得到过零花钱吗？

关于给小孩补助或零花钱的价值，仁者见仁，智者见智。在这一点上，你可能会发现你的父母也需要一点点说服力。其实，你的父母或许心知肚明，他们相信，你在幼年时就开始学会管理自己的钱是非常重要的。

你得到过多少零花钱？

你能得到的零花钱的多少，取决于你的父母能给你的数目，或者取决于他们认为你应该得到多少。

请你记住，你的父母一切都希望给你最好的，请你像接受礼物一样接受你父母给你的零花钱。事实就是如此！即使你的父母给你的零花钱少之又少，你也应当心存感激。

父母备忘录

* 让你们的孩子拥有零花钱，对你们的孩子大有裨益。

* 它有助于培养你们的孩子的独立意识。

* 它能够帮助你们的孩子理解金钱的价值。

* 它能够教会你们的孩子做出决定，是直接把它花掉，还是把它存起来，或者几个星期后用它去购买一件特别的东西。

年龄和阶段

在你们的孩子的每个生日到来的时候，你们都应该定额地增加孩子的零花钱。如果你们的孩子已经长大了，大到可以帮助你们干家务活，那么，你们就可以安排他参与家务劳动，作为交换，你们可以给他一些额外的零花钱。

家务活

因为你负责完成了某项家务活,作为回报,你的父母可能会额外给你一个星期的零花钱。你不可能永远生活在一个饭来张口、衣来伸手的世界中,因此通过劳动获得收入是一种很好的锻炼,这是为你的将来做准备的。

附带条件

因此,随着零花钱而来的是责任心。如果你获取零花钱的附带条件是你必须完成某项家务活,那么,你就有必要与你的父母签订一份协议或合同,在协议或合同中应该明确规定你父母期望你完成的事项。

小工作,大影响

家务活可能是很简单的,或许只是让你在厨房里帮忙,也可能只是让你打扫自己的房间——这本来就是你应该做的!他们也可能会让你去照顾宠物,还可能会让你清洗汽车或者在花园里干活。

你所做的这些家务活一定是可以帮到你的父母的,并且一定是全部家务活中的一部分。

合同

为什么预先签订一份合同或协议是非常重要的？一旦你同意做什么家务活可以得到报酬，做什么家务活不能得到报酬，那么，你的父母便会希望你能够坚持下去，遵守约定。当你无法按约定做好你的事情时，麻烦便会随之而来，比如说，你忘记了铺床，忘记关掉楼下的电灯，或者把猫关在了门外。

按协议在家里做一些有意义的家务活，它能够让你获得更多的零花钱

针锋相对（以牙还牙）

当然，你的父母也可能会认为，你帮助他们做家务应该是你日常生活的一部分，他们并不乐意为此支付给你报酬。

你能做的工作

清洗车库	聚会表演	照看老奶奶和老爷爷
给花园家具和围栏上油漆	做小丑、魔术师	送货
做园丁	制作气球模型	电脑设计
洗车	讲故事，表演	制作卡片、标志等
铲雪	音乐制作	工厂销售
扫地，擦窗	动物收容所工作人员	在小花盆里种植草本植物
骑术学校帮手	清洁犬舍，遛狗，喂食	卖旧衣服、玩具、游戏机
照看植物	宠物保姆	设计T恤衫

赚 钱

过不了多久,你就会明白,让你有钱的最可靠的方法是赚钱。或许你得到零花钱和一些补贴是有附带条件的,比如说,你得做一些零星的家务活才能换回一两美元的零花钱。但是,进入劳动力市场,也就是走出家门出售你自己的时间、精力和专业知识,不仅会给你带来收入,而且还会让你受益匪浅。

第一份工作

几乎可以肯定,你的第一份工作必定是在"做好功课"的前提下接受的。不要低估任何一份工作的要求。如果你接受了某份工作,你就必须全力以赴地花时间去完成它。你必须优先把这项工作做好,就像在学校里一样。

再者,你又不想放弃你的体育活动、社交活动以及家庭生活,所以完成这项工作是需要花费你额外的精力和时间的。为此,在你接受这份工作之前,请务必三思!

承担固定工作能够为你赚取额外补贴

付出努力会得到回报

最后,你会因为你付出的努力和做出的贡献而获得回报——这应该会使你感觉良好!你会因此而获得真正的成就感,你的自信心也会得到增强!

儿童消费力

通过"儿童消费力",孩子们在很大程度上实现了对家庭支出的控制。"儿童消费力"是指儿童说服父母花钱的能力。英国有超过三分之二的青少年说,他们有能力去影响父母的购买决策,他们能够让父母对他们言听计从……

研究人员发现,父母不喜欢对孩子们说"不",他们情愿放弃购买自己的东西,也不愿意拒绝孩子们的要求。

当你有钱时的三种选择

在你让它发挥作用之前，钱只不过是一块金属或一张纸，甚至有可能只是一张塑料卡。你可以以三种不同的方式去使用它：你可以花掉它，也可以把它存起来，或者把它捐给别人。不同的使用方法会给你带来不同的结果。

• • • • • • • • • • •

花掉它

对于那些喜欢花钱的人来说，钱是有史以来最好的东西。它是支持你长时间购物以及拥有物品（而且是新的物品）的关键所在。不过，它会让你养成一个坏习惯，即纯粹为购物而购物。

当然，钱也可以让你获得新的体验、让你去冒险，它可以让你有实力加入某个俱乐部，帮助你签订对你有利的合同。如果你能够明智地花钱，那么，你就会拥有这些新财富或新体验给你带来的好处。

存起来

有些人可以轻轻松松地把钱存起来,这实在让人惊讶。对他们来说,这似乎是件很自然的事。人们处理金钱的方式是很不一样的,一如他们的外表,以及别的他们感兴趣的事情一样。

你只需要不花掉你赚来的或者得到的钱,你便能够存下钱来。如果你手上只有几枚硬币,那么,你就可以将它存在储钱罐里。但是当你得到了更多的钱时,你就会希望把它存在银行里,这样你每个月还会获得一笔额外的收入——利息。

捐给别人

与他人分享是你通常会做的一件事,这只是因为你想这样做,而不是因为你必须这样做。你对你的朋友伸出援助之手,可能是因为你知道在某个时候你的朋友会回报于你。但实际上,帮助那些急需帮助的人,会让你感觉良好。我们的周围有很多人都急需别人的帮助。每星期都往慈善箱里投进几枚硬币,意味着在某个地方的某个人将会受到你的帮助。当然,你也可以直接帮助那些需要帮助的人,这样,你就能看到你的资助是如何帮到他们的。

存起来

对很多人来说,存钱就像花钱一样容易。有些人甚至说,存钱就是花钱的对立面。从表面上看起来或许确实如此,但实际上并非如此。你可能会说,与往你口袋里装进10英镑钱相反的是从你口袋里拿走了10英镑钱。不过,事情真的就这么简单吗?

睡着了的现金

如果存钱对你来说意味着把现金藏到你的床垫底下,并且让它静静地躺在那儿,那么,你就会发现,随着时间的推移,被你"藏"起来的钱的价值会不断地下降。如果你把它扔进你的储钱罐,它一样也只是静静地待在那儿毫无作为。因此,这类存钱方式都不可能是你想要的。

工作着的现金

与上面所说的相反,另外还有几种存钱方式,从根本上说,它们与花钱一样,也是把你的钱投入流通当中去。当你把你的钱存入你的银行或邮局的储蓄账户时,你要相信别人会让你的钱越变越多。银行会把你的钱投资到商业交易中,它会设法赚取利润,而其中的一部分利润会以利息的方式返还给你。

你是哪类储蓄者？

非储蓄者

* 你花钱时完全不考虑你需要什么以及想要什么。
* 你总是会买一些稀奇古怪的奢侈品，因此一分钱也存不下来。
* 你总是入不敷出。

小额储蓄者

* 你很会花钱，不过你会衡量一下你需要什么和想要什么。
* 也许你不会购买一些稀奇古怪的奢侈品，因此你可以节省下一点点钱。
* 你存下来的钱会慢慢地增多。
* 你存的钱越多，你的感觉越好。
* 你仍然会购买一些你想要的东西。
* 你能够应对突发事件。
* 你会购买一些即使用你一个星期或者一个月的零花钱也买不起的东西。
* 你正在学习某些生活技能。

储蓄大赢家

* 你尽可能地少花钱。
* 你很喜欢存钱，平常只购买一些必需品。
* 你尽可能多地把钱存入银行。

小猪储钱罐

大多数孩子都可能曾经拥有过一个小猪储钱罐。但是,为什么是小猪储钱罐呢?为什么不是小犀牛储钱罐,或者小土豚储钱罐呢?难道是人们认为小猪比其他动物更能够让人们节省自己辛苦赚来的钱吗?好吧,或许如此,但是这并不是我们拥有小猪储钱罐的原因。

把小猪养肥

在很久很久以前,在西方社会,猪是穷人们的储钱罐。春天,穷人们从市场上买回一头小猪,每天喂给它吃家里的剩菜剩饭,把它养大养肥,然后在入冬之前把它宰杀掉。你的小猪储钱罐是用你节省下来的零花钱喂养的,同样也能把它养肥。当储钱罐被塞满钱时,你就可以打碎它,把里面的钱取出来了。

在德语国家里,付工资给学徒是一种惯例,学徒是指那些为了成为技工而接受培训的人,学徒们一年的工资通常就是一头猪。因此,猪便成了投资的象征——既是金钱投资的象征,也是投资年轻人的象征!

Pyggs(储钱罐)

很久以前,人们在厨房里摆满了各式各样由一种被称为 pygg 的黏土做成的瓶瓶罐罐。当他们想要存一些钱时,为了安全起见,他们就把钱放到这些瓶瓶罐罐里去。最后,这些存放钱的瓶瓶罐罐就被人们称为"pygg 储钱罐"了,后来又进一步被称为"pyggy 储钱罐"。

毫无疑问,没过多久,一些精明的手工艺人从中获得了灵感,于是就制做出了形状像一头真正的猪的储钱罐,小猪储钱罐就这样诞生了。

古老的黏土 pygg 储钱罐

我们今天所熟知的小猪储钱罐

银行里的钱

你现在有一些钱了,假设你已经决定不把它们放到储钱罐里,也不把它们藏到床垫底下,那么,现在你的这些钱足够开一个银行账户吗?当你新开一个账户时,银行通常会希望你在这个账户上存有一个最低限度的金额,以使它认为它给你开设这个银行账户是值得的。如果你账户上的钱太少,以至于小于银行要求的最低金额,那么,你就可能要为保有这个账户而交一点"罚金"了。所以,这是你要弄清楚的第一件事情。

这对你来说意味着什么?

银行可能会要求一个最低存款额。

作为交换,你得到的是:
* 一个存放你现金的地方。
* 一个投资你现金的地方。
* 一个带息的储蓄账户(关于利息的相关内容,请参见第27页)。
* 一张借记卡,它能够在ATM(自动取款机)上提取现金,也能够在商店里进行刷卡消费。
* 甚至你还有可能会收到一两件免费的礼物。银行一直都在寻找新的年轻的客户。

你的年龄足够大了吗?

最大的问题是年龄。在许多国家,如果你想拥有一个你自己的银行账户,你必须年满18周岁,或者达到国家规定的其他法定年龄。但是如果你没达到法定年龄,也请不要灰心丧气,你的父母能够帮你获得一个你自己的账户,但这并不意味着这个账户是属于你父母的——你有隐私权,银行信件是寄给你的。

银行账户

在线账户（网上银行）

一般情况下，银行会为你开通在线账户（网上银行），因此，你可以随时随地查询你的银行余额和关注你的投资情况。

活期存款账户

所有银行都会为你提供一个活期存款账户——一个允许你自由存取钱的账户。当然，你也随时可以撤销账户。不过这种账户，你是得不到一分利息的，因为你的存款金额随时都会发生变动。然而，有些银行规定，如果存款余额达到了某个点，它还是会为存款人的活期账户支付利息的。因此，在你开设账户之前，你最好先了解一下。你应该要求银行每月都给你寄一份账单，或者让你能够在网上查询。

储蓄账户

为了确保你的钱能不断地"生钱"，你需要开设一个储蓄账户。储蓄账户种类繁多，这取决于你想要存放多少钱以及存多久。很显然，如果你把你的现金存放在银行里越久，那么，银行给你回报的利息就会越多。

越来越多的钱

对于钱来说，它最大的一个特点是本身的票面价值是不会丧失的。如果你的床垫底下放了 5 英镑，那么，当你隔很久以后把它取出来时，它仍然是 5 英镑。它虽然可能已经买不了当初那么多的东西了，但是它仍然是 5 英镑。

当你花钱买东西的时候，你要知道，世事多变，商品是会贬值的。那么，"贬值"是什么意思呢？它意味着随着时间的推移，你付钱买来的东西的价值开始下降了。有时候有些东西越老旧越不值钱。

在某种程度上，钱和物品是一样的：物品越陈旧，越不值钱，钱也是如此。物价的上涨只会使同样的钱买到更少的物品，这样，钱的价值就变小了。

对付这一切的唯一办法是，让你的钱越来越多。

赚取利息

当你把钱存入银行的储蓄账户时，你希望你的钱会越变越多。这是因为银行利用你的钱去做业务投资了，它要给你支付使用费，这个使用费就是利息。

利息是支付给贷款人的利润或报酬。利息让人很感兴趣，因为任何人都可以获得利息，让人们的钱变多一点点，有时候会多很多。

单利是指在你原有的存款金额的基础上计算利息，以下这张表格里所列的内容就是单利的计算情况。当你在银行里存入1英镑，存期5年，利息率是10%。

年份	总投资	利息率	单利计算
1	1英镑	10%	1.1英镑
2			1.2英镑
3			1.3英镑
4			1.4英镑
5			1.5英镑

复利支付比单利更划算。利息率是一样的，存款的时间也是相同的，但是利息是按照总存款金额来计算的。利息也能赚钱，它能让你的钱生钱生得更快。以下表格是复利计算情况。

年份	总投资	利息率	复利计算
1	1英镑	10%	1.1英镑
2			1.21英镑
3			1.33英镑
4			1.46英镑
5			1.61英镑

你可以赚取利息，无论是复利还是单利。

花掉它

人人都爱花钱。花钱会让我们得到我们想要的东西,这让我们感觉非常美好。其实这并不难!只要你想花钱,这世界上从来都不会缺乏让你花钱的东西。但是如果你真想买东西而又确实没有主意时,你可以看看街上、杂志上、电视上,甚至是印在你的购物袋上的那些铺天盖地的广告。

明智地花钱

但是我们必须有责任地花钱。你只能花你手头上拥有的钱。如果你小心谨慎地花钱,一切都会安然无恙;如果你花钱大手大脚,不计后果,那么,你最终会让自己陷入麻烦当中。

钱的价值

当你的父母教训你,要你明白钱的价值时,实际上他们的意思是,要你知道如何明智地花钱。

你是哪类花钱者?

不会花钱者

* 你会把每一分钱都存起来。
* 你宁愿什么也没有,或者什么都凑合着用,也不愿意拿你的宝贵的现金去购买东西。
* 你什么也不花,让你的钱不断变多。

小心谨慎的花钱者

* 你会花钱,但在花钱之前你会仔细衡量你需要什么以及你想要什么。
* 或许你没有购买那些稀奇古怪的奢侈品的习惯,因此你能够节省下一点钱。
* 你节省下来的钱会积少成多。

大手大脚的花钱者

* 你不断地花钱,最后花得一分不剩。
* 你感觉很好,你看起来也很好,你拥有的物品堆积如山。
* 在你的朋友看来,你是一个"大人物",是一个成功人士。
* 你口袋里装满了钱,它让你看上去充满了力量——可惜只是暂时的。
* 当这一切都烟消云散时,你从天堂跌入了地狱。
* 你将一无所有,无从应对突发事件。
* 你再也得不到你一直以来梦寐以求的东西,因为你已经买不起了。
* 你已经超支了,有时候你还不得不举债度日。

买东西（购物）

大多数消费都发生在商店里。今天，商店是一个极具现代化且令人目眩神迷的地方，商店里的商品琳琅满目，既富感染力，又让人爱不释手。但这只是近些年才发展起来的。

商店的发展

商店的发展历史很悠久，最早的时候，小商贩们或挑担提货，或牵着小马驹，走街串巷地吆喝买卖。

商店最早起始于主要街道上的露天交易，那时卖主寥寥无几，他们可能是一个屠夫，也可能是一个面包师，抑或是一个烛台制作者。

你的祖父母或者你的太祖父母一定还记得，在他们那个年代，服装店很少，没有出售光盘和唱片的音乐商店，当然更没有销售蒸汽熨斗和电视机的电器商店。

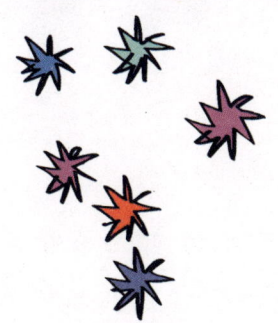

商店里的物品

你曾经期望在杂货店里买到金鱼吃的食物吗？在纸店里买到小发卡吗？在汽车修理厂里买到报纸吗？这些事情看起来似乎很奇怪，但它确实发生了。越来越多的商店都把它们的存货限定在那些最畅销的商品上。

一家商店能够出售各种各样的商品。有些老式的街角小店储存了当地社区所需要的所有商品。有些商店，比如说加油站商店，店主们知道，一旦你把车子停下来，走出汽车，便希望尽可能快地完成购物。

便利购物是新的发展方向。人们工作的时间越来越长了，而用于购物的时间却越来越少。无论你是本地人还是外地人，便利店外观给人的感觉都是差不多的，而里面销售的东西也大同小异。

价格

价格是很重要的。人们通常会对自己的支出定一个限额，如果他们在一种商品上花费多了，那么在另外一种商品上的花费就会变少。

当一种商品的价格上涨时，另一种价格更便宜的竞争性商品就会变得畅销起来。与每公斤2英镑的汉堡相比，人们更愿意购买每公斤1英镑的汉堡。

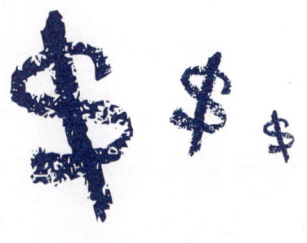

去购物

你最喜欢哪家商店或商铺？你肯定会有几家自己喜欢的商店。关于我们的购物习惯的一个最令人惊讶的事实是，我们总是倾向于一遍又一遍地光顾少数几家自己最喜欢的商店，而很少改变自己的购物模式。我们喜欢这些商店陈列商品的方式，喜欢它们销售的物品，或许我们还喜欢它们的员工。

我们喜欢这样。当我们在逛商店时，那里的一切都是我们所期望的。我们不需要惊喜，我们只要感觉舒服就可以了。商店的设计人员知道这一点，因此他们尽量对商店的布局不做大的变动，这样我们就一直会拥有一种宾至如归的感觉。

购物氛围

不同商店的布局千差万别，从堆满盒子和物品的杂货店，到装有许许多多低光照明灯的、亮光闪闪的、布置简洁的手机店，五花八门，各式各样的都有。无论商店做何种装饰，店家无非是想营造一个最佳的购物氛围。

生活情调

如果商店销售的是那种强调生活情调的商品，那么，它可能会拥有一个更宽敞的过道，布置成冷色调，只在比较显眼的地方摆放一些经过精挑细选的物品，以及一两把坐椅，并伴以轻柔的音乐，这些会让你感到很奢华。

熟悉感

我们每个人都只会到少数几家自己喜欢的商店去购物。在逛街时，我们总是会重复相同的路线，总是对一些商店视而不见，总是走进那些早已非常熟悉的商店；即使有新的门店开张了，我们也很少会改变自己的购物习惯。我们知道自己喜欢什么。

购物点

色彩缤纷的购物点吸引了你的注意力

我们一遍又一遍地去同一家商店购物

这里说的购物点是指商店内的购物地点,有时也被称为销售点,它是你接触商品的地方。具体地说,它指商店里的某个放置商品的货架。但是所有物品的摆放都是随机的吗?或许它们只是你碰巧停下来的时候被你看到并被你选中的吗?当然不是!

店家知道,多达四分之三的物品都是被那些随意闲逛商店的人买去的。他们花在每个货架上的时间只有10秒钟,因此,每件物品都必须摆放在合适的位置上,必须在人们的视线范围内,而且还必须在人们触手可及的地方。这些物品的包装必须能够吸引顾客的眼球。

购物同时也是一种娱乐消遣。有些商店采用独立式陈列,它意味着你必须绕着商品走,或者要走到商品的背面,或许你还得抬起头来或俯下身子去看。这是一种捉迷藏式的设计,它会让你备感兴趣,让你充满遐想。

让购物变成一种乐趣吧!

整洁的橱窗陈设吸引了经验丰富的买家

物美价廉的商品

我们都喜欢物美价廉的商品，没有什么会比买到这类商品更让人感觉良好了。如果你为了能够买到便宜一点的商品，为了找到减价商品或者特惠商品，愿意多花点时间一家一家商店地去搜寻，那么买到便宜的物品并不难。

有很多地方可以找到它们！

因破产而打折甩卖的物品

破产公司所销售的物品，通常都是破产公司自己的正品。这将是一桩不错的买卖，但是请你一定不要忘记核实你有没有获得保证——当物品需要修理或者销售员弄错了需要更换时的一种保证。你必须弄清楚，他们有没有多余的零部件可供替换，因为制造商并不在当地，可能无法及时更换出了故障的商品的零部件。

小摊贩

街头小摊贩总是把摊点摆在街角，卖的东西似乎与商店里的东西是一样的——除了他们的东西特别便宜之外。但请你记住，如果你基于某一理由想退回商品时，这些摊贩第二天未必依然会在那里。除了这种风险之外，街头小摊贩的好处是，能够为你提供良好的交易，他们销售清仓货物，或者从已经倒闭的公司那里进货。

网上购物

　　网上购物应该会更便宜，毕竟在商品的价格中不必包含门店成本，也不需要高楼大厦和销售人员。但网上购物最大的问题在于，商品的照片看起来比商品本身更具诱惑力，实际商品的颜色可能与你在照片上看起来的有些不同，面料会让你失望，等等。如果发生这种情况，你可以选择退回你不喜欢的商品。但是，请记住，拆封商品时一定要小心，因为如果你想获得全额退款，你得按原样原封不动地重新把商品包装好。你还得保存退货记录。

直销店

　　直销店是近些年才出现的廉价购物场所。每类商品的设计者和制造商每年都会改变他们的设计和库存物品，有时候甚至一年还不止一次。因为老产品必须为新产品让路。直销店往往专营设计师的品牌和季节性的时尚用品，这些用品会被嵌入一个智能标签，因此，即使你购买的商品已经被用了一个季节了，但智能标签仍能体现这件商品的独特性。

慈善商店

　　慈善商店里满是便宜的商品。它们只销售获赠的最优质的商品，商店里面可能什么都有。你购买店里的商品，就等于是你在做好事。每一家慈善商店实际上都是在为某一事件筹集资金，你每一次小小的购买其实都是对慈善事业的贡献。

被迫购买

随着你年龄的增大，被迫购买的情形会日渐增多，有些可能是来自于你想购买的商品的公司，还有些可能来自于已经买了商品的你的朋友。生产商需要做广告，以告知消费者有关产品的信息。有些广告也是劝说性的，以劝说消费者购买它的商品。有些广告则是诱导性的，它让你觉得你有必要购买它的商品，而实际上你根本就不需要。

"圈子成员"

广告商相信你是喜新厌旧的。他们认为你不会忠诚于任何一个品牌，你会改变你的消费倾向，把目光转移到任何一个更酷的或者更为时尚的商品上。你是这样的吗？

广告商运用广告的技法十分巧妙，几乎所有的广告或多或少地都会运用一些手法。广告会适时地告诉你，如果你不买它推广的商品，那么你便落伍了，你不再是"圈子里的一员"了，并且除你之外，其他人都做出了正确的选择，而只有你却一无所知。

但是，请你做那个特立独行的人吧！你只购买那些你需要的东西吧！虽然那些广告中的产品是那么的与众不同，也是那么的新奇。

请认真权衡广告上的产品……并做出自己的选择。

来自同龄人的压力

抵制同龄人的压力并没有那么容易。在日常生活中，我们需要社会认同感，模仿同学和朋友，翻看时尚杂志，通过别人对你的言行举止来判断自己，所有这些都是我们渴望获得社会认同的表现。你必须鼓起勇气，让自己在人群中脱颖而出，做适合自己做的事。

做你自己

我们要做最适合自己做的事，穿适合自己穿的衣服，表达自己的观点，只做自己，不要让自己成为别人的翻版。

请你务必记住，说到底，世界各地的制造商、零售商和广告商，都是以"你"为模型的，然后让别人来模仿"你"。他们是通过创造大众时尚、塑造大众态度以及引导大众购买潮流而赚钱的。

成为"圈子里的一员"会让你有舒适感，但是请你不要让自己受同龄人太多的影响。

铺天盖地而来的信息

为了让你乖乖地掏出钱，广告商们每年都会花上数十亿美元来做广告，而你每年都会看到成千上万个广告。这对你来说是一个巨大的压力。一般的青少年在15岁之前大约会收到包括广告在内的大约25万条媒体信息。

真是浪费

你的衣柜里到底有多少条牛仔裤、有多少件T恤衫和衬衫,以及其他从未穿过的衣服?有可能它们从来都未曾被你取下过衣架吧?我们购买东西时的理由各式各样,但是很少是因为我们缺少和需要它们。更有可能是基于其他的某个理由,而且在很多时候,这个理由可能是毫无道理的。

选不胜选

如果你想要一个巧克力棒,摆在你面前可供选择的品种会有20种之多。需要一份早餐麦片吗?品种有12个。羊毛衫的款式,有100种。杂志呢?依然如此。食品、服装、娱乐,品种繁多,五花八门,让我们选不胜选。

回到过去的"好"时光……

曾经有一段时间,这些东西被认为是我们生活的必需品。然而,事实上,在第二次世界大战结束之后的一段时间里,也就是在20世纪50年代,你必须持有购物证才能购买商品。也许你的某位家人还记得这些事。这并非是很久以前的事。但是如今,随着世界各国的物品不断互相涌入各国,物品早已过剩,大家再也不用为了一条冬季短裤而排队了。

购物狂

相比于那个限额配给的"著名的"年代，毫无疑问，现在的我们已经被宠坏了。我们所有人几乎都是购物狂。我们浪费成性，因为物品已经不再是新的了，我们便毫不吝啬地随意丢弃。我们扔掉食物，并不是因为它们已经变质了，而是因为我们有了更新鲜的食物。我们扔掉衬衫，是因为把它送到干洗店去清洗比重新买一件更贵。

过度消费

在许多发达国家，不少人已经成了"专家级"的消费者，他们一方面过度购买，另一方面又会毫不犹豫地扔掉一些他们购买来的物品。据统计，在英国，人们扔掉了他们购买的食物的30%。一个事实是，我们大家都太过于浪费了！

堆积如山的废弃物

借钱与债务

然而，不管你怎么努力来计划你的预算，还总是会出现钱不够花的时候。当你急需用钱时，你却已经把钱花光了，这就会产生一个问题，即你必须请求别人的帮助。你必须找到一个愿意借钱给你的人，并且是在条件不太苛刻的情况下借到钱。

向朋友借钱

朋友比其他人更有可能借钱给你——无息贷款。换句话说，你还给朋友的钱跟你向朋友借的钱的数额是一样的，不需要支付额外的利息。不过话虽如此，但任何借款都是举债，举债终归是一个不受欢迎的坏习惯。

当你向朋友借钱时，你的朋友可能顺带请求你帮他一个小忙，当然，你很难拒绝这样的要求。

总之，请你记住，即使借钱这种事只是偶尔为之，那也是一种债务，而不是一份礼物。当其中一方欠债不还时，时常会危及双方的友谊，并最终导致两人关系的破裂。

向父母借钱

就像偶尔向朋友借钱一样,你或许偶尔也会向你的父母借钱,不过并不总是如此。依据借款金额的多少,你需要与你的父母协商好,借多少就还多少,而且还要约定什么时候归还。

并且还要记住,如果你不履行自己的承诺,那么,你将再也无法从你的父母那里借到更多的钱,或者得到他们的帮助和救济。对此,你的父母会郑重地告诉你,你没有第二次机会了。他们当然是正确的!如果你已经有胆量向他们借钱了,那么,你肯定已经长大到足以能够承担还款的责任了。

你的父母可能会向你收取利息,不一定是金钱方面的利息,他们可能会要求你做一些额外的家务活或者学会某项礼仪。

借钱和信贷

或许现在你仍然处在向父母要零花钱的年龄阶段，我们在这个时候警告你有关债务的危险，似乎是一种奇怪的做法。不过，我们这里的主要目的并不是给你一个建议，而是让你意识到举债的后果。

明白借钱的后果

太多人都陷入了债务越来越多导致的困境当中，因为他们没有意识到，一旦他们欠债了，事情就会变得更为艰难。如果欠债不还，信用卡公司和银行就会向借款人施加压力，他们有可能再也无法向它们寻求帮助了。所以，如果你现在就意识到举债的后果是什么，那么将来当你需要借钱的时候，你可能就会仔细思量了。

无法还清的借款

债务只有在你没有能力还款时，才会成为一个问题，因此，无论如何你都要避免这种情形出现，即使这意味着你无法得到你所要的东西也如此。

当事情真正变得非常糟糕的时候，便会有被人们称为收债人的人到你家里来了，他们会搬走所有你支付不起的东西……想象一下，那会有多么糟糕！

欠债——困难的事儿

当你向某人或者某公司借钱时,债务便发生了。

借钱的唯一诀窍是,必须保证过一段时间你能够还清你所欠的钱;如果你不能做到每个月都有足够的钱来还款,那么,请你不要借债。这看起来似乎很容易做到,但是很多人却做不到——很多时候这并不是他们的错。任何举债都是有风险的,因此,你应该把风险降到最低程度。

什么是负债?

负债的结果有可能是相当糟糕的:
* 你总是焦虑不安。
* 你无法随心所欲地花钱。
* 你所有的余钱都将用来支付一些费用或者逐日增多的债务利息。
* 你看不到出头之日。

什么是信用额度?

信用额度是指固定金额的贷款。贷方决定贷给你多少钱,这取决于你的个人财务价值和净资产状况。与其他所借的款项一样,你同样可以花费你所贷来的款项,但是你也必须偿还贷款。如果贷方没什么问题的话,那么,你偿还贷款也不会有太多麻烦。不过,许多公司都陷入了麻烦。一些信贷方贷出的款额太多了。这样问题就来了。

做好预算

做好预算

做好预算是最简单的理财方式。它并不是最令人激动的事情之一。实际上，消费，甚至是储蓄给人带来的感觉，都远远胜过预算。但是预算是那种会变得越来越简单的事情之一（一旦你开始做了）。

预算就像是去看牙医。这是一个艰难的选择，但你知道它对你有好处。

我能负担得起吗？

做预算意味着你承认你的货币来源是有限的，这并不是一件好玩的事。这也表明你很清楚，你想要做的事情远远多于你负担得起的事情。

一个好消息是，一旦你做好了预算，无论你如何花费，你都不会感到焦虑，而且你的钱也都会花在刀刃上。

是的，我能！

如果你做好了预算，几乎可以肯定地表明，你会有足够的钱去做一些你想做的事情。你可能必须花一些时间存钱来实现你的愿望，甚至可能还要再多等一些时间。你可能不得不分批地购买你想要的东西，而不是一次性地把想买的东西全部买下，比如说，你的CD集或者你冬天穿的衣服。

不，我不能！

让你推迟做某件你想做的事，或者推迟购买你认为你必须买的东西，并不是一件容易的事。因为我们生活在一个事后兑现承诺的世界中：现在就买吧，然后再考虑付款的事情；用信用卡就行了，等账单到了再考虑怎么还款……

如果你是这样做的，那么几乎可以肯定地说，你会因为这种没有预算的糟糕习惯而受苦受累。当然，你或许可以找人来帮你，因为你还小，或者你并不知道怎样才是更好的，但是不幸的是，世事难料。在现实世界中，那个唯一能帮助你的人可能会向你索取一大笔钱。

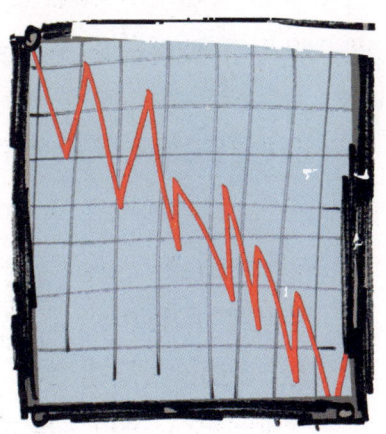

首先，预算需要自律。

统计结果如何？

吞世代青少年

青少年（13～15岁）特别精明。他们收到的钱多，花的也多，他们试图拥有隐私，想摆脱家长的束缚，想从规则和日常规范中解放出来。他们生活的重点是寻求乐趣、追求时尚和交友。

被称为"吞世代"（8～12岁）的数以百万计的群体，比以往任何时候都具有更强大的消费力。这是因为他们的父母往往都忙于工作，会给他们很多钱，以此来减轻自己的负疚感。以下是关于吞世代的一些统计数据：

* 平均津贴为每周8英镑。
* 吞世代喜欢装老成，也希望自己看起来更成熟，像他们的哥哥和姐姐，他们也倾向于使用更成熟的产品。

* 他们热爱手机。

移动世界

手机是吞世代朋友之间保持联系、玩游戏以及找到最新时尚配饰的宠儿。

* 目前全世界有超过10亿部手机。
* 在英国，有60%的年轻人（100万）拥有自己的手机或被准许使用他们父母的手机。
* 现在拥有一部自己的手机的平均年龄为14岁。
* 短信是吞世代交流的高端方式。

向你发送广告

* 你通常会在晚上或者每周六早上的某一特定时间看电视吗？
* 你认为以你为目标顾客的广告太多了吗？
* 你认为以你为目标顾客的有关甜食和快餐的广告太多了吗？

嗯，你的回答应该是肯定的！

时刻都有一大批统计人员在关注着你,他们记录着你的一切:你消费了多少,在哪儿消费的。这是因为你花得太多了。你对你所生活的国家的经济做出了巨大的贡献,因此零售商们和制造商们想知道你的一切。

挥金如土者

你所花的钱(每年2 300美元)的大部分(60%)来自于你的零花钱或补贴。其余的则来自于你做家务所得,或者你以礼物的方式得到的,或者是你打零工所得。

* 但是,谁花的钱最多?是女孩吗?抑或是男孩?
* 谁最会节约用钱?是女孩吗?抑或是男孩?

第一个问题的答案是女孩。女孩每个星期的花费都要超过13英镑,而男孩每个星期的花费则只要11英镑多。

你的钱都花到什么地方去了?

* 你三分之二的钱都花在了糖果和巧克力上。
* 女孩们把剩下的钱都花在了衣服、鞋子、杂志和化妆品上了。
* 男孩们则把剩下的钱都用在了更多的食物和饮料、电脑游戏、视频和CD上了。

你的选择

你最喜欢把钱花在哪方面,请在以下选项中打勾:

* 电影/音乐会。
* 衣服。
* 糖果和零食。
* 鞋子,包括运动鞋。
* 电脑游戏。
* 体育赛事。
* 书籍。
* 移动电话和手机卡。
* 杂志。
* 化妆品和化妆用具。
* CD、影片。
* 其他。

上述事项你都做过预算了吗?当你看到一双昂贵的运动鞋时,你会:

* 把钱存起来,直到你买得起为止。
* 通过做家务挣钱。
* 缠着父母要额外的现金。
* 要求作为生日礼物提前送给你。

你能从你的答案中领悟到什么吗?

把钱捐给别人

世界上需要我们帮助的人有很多很多。如果你经常看电视上的新闻报道，或者浏览报纸上的"求助"栏目，那么你必定意识到了，生活于贫困的国家或者饱受战乱的国家的人们，生活是如何的艰难。如果你打算关心世事或者关心那些求助于你的人，如果你打算成为一个"地球公民"，而不是一个冷漠的消极被动的人，那么现在就是你该关注这些事情的时候了。

因为战争或灾难逃离家园的难民们，他们住在临时搭建的棚户里，直到能够返家那天为止

需要帮助的儿童每人分得一箱来自海外援助的餐点

每一个小小的帮助

我们每个人都有需求和欲望。需求是指我们对那些生活必需品的需要，比如说对食物、水、衣物等。欲望是指我们对那些我们认为它们是我们必不可少的东西的需要，比如说冰淇淋、电子游戏和名牌服装等。但是，即使没有这些能够满足我们欲望的东西，我们也一样能够生活下去，因此，我们有能力去帮助别人。当你看到难民们的照片，知道了他们的悲惨经历时，你可能根本不知道应该如何去帮助他们。

但是，事实上，每个人的每一个小小的帮助都确实能发挥作用。

帮助国外的穷人

我们每天都能听到一些有关可怕的贫穷和饥饿的国外新闻。当你听到这些新闻时，可能只是耸耸肩，觉得这是别人的事，与你毫不相干——毕竟这些离你太遥远了，而且你会想他们国家的政府为什么不帮助他们。

但是，当少数人拥有大量的钱，而大部分人却在为他们的生活而乞讨时，这事儿似乎就不怎么和谐了，有可能需要我们去改变些什么。我们每个人都能够为此贡献自己小小的力量，要知道，积少成多，众志成城。

无家可归的人

即使在富裕的国家里，也还是有许多无家可归的人。请为慈善事业做点贡献吧！帮助那些无家可归的人，让他们不再露宿街头，给他们一个容身之地吧！

感觉很棒

给那些生活不如你的人捐款，并不是为了让你感到自己很神圣，或者让你感到沾沾自喜。而是让你明白，因为你的给予，世界上某个地方的某个人今天有了一口饭吃。

这样，你就会觉得你做了一件有意义的事情。

慈善机构

伸出援助之手

慈善机构是这样一些组织，它们以各种方式去帮助那些处于困难中的人。你可能已经听说过许多著名的慈善机构，或许你可能还偶尔得到过它们的帮助呢！

如果你第一时间奔赴灾区，紧急救援需要救助的人，并同时长期为灾区工作，改善当地的教育和医疗卫生状况，那么，这还会给你带来良好的声誉。

基金会

基金会也是慈善机构，它们是由一些资金雄厚的公司、个人或家庭提供资金，为支持某些项目而设立的。各种基金会都可以把特定的资金用于慈善事业。这些基金会的收入不需要缴纳税收，因此它们和你捐款的钱可以全部拿来做慈善事业。

筹集资金

你可以发起慈善步行活动。在这样一个慈善赞助活动中,你必须围绕当地公园和较偏远的树林行走。你每走一公里,各种各样的朋友和家庭就会赞助你,金额是每公里10便士。你可以作为某个慈善小组中的一员,也可以与你的家人一起步行,当然,你还可以与你的同学一起参加这个活动。如果除你之外还有另外50个人与你同时在做这件事……那么,你们所筹得的款项将会是一笔大数额。

你应该捐赠多少钱,这完全由你自己决定,你当然应该选择一个让你感到舒服的数额。不过,请你记住,万丈高楼平地起,无论你捐的金额多么少,只要你定期捐助,你的捐助都将会变得非常有意义。

而且不要忘记,捐钱只不过是帮助别人的一种方式而已,你还可以捐玩具、书籍和衣服给这些慈善机构,所有这一切都将对有需要的人有所帮助。

富裕与贫穷

很多人认为,如果他们更富有,那他们会更快乐。诚然,衣食富足、生活无忧的人,比那些衣不蔽体、食不果腹、贫困潦倒的人更幸福。但是,一旦你已经过上了舒适的生活,那么是不是更多的钱会带来更多的快乐呢?自然,富有并不能保证幸福,富有并不是得到快乐的唯一途径。

为财富而奋斗?

伟大的印度领袖莫罕达斯·甘地认为,幸福来自于简单的生活。就像那些信奉佛教的人一样,他以拒绝财富作为实现他人生信条的一种手段,他甚至自己动手缝制衣服。

那些认为幸福会随财富而来的人发现,他们自己正艰难地爬在一个上升的斜坡上,他们为了让自己更加富有,正不断地奋斗,但却因为爬不上顶点而变得越来越不快乐。最后,他们觉得自己就像是一个失败者,因为他们永远也站不到最高处。他们不知道,知足是幸福的钥匙。

有了一切之后

一个人收入的多少，决定了他们可以购买的物品的数量的多少。如果一个低收入者决定花1 000英镑到世界各地去旅行，那么，他将不得不在衣、食、住等方面削减开支。但是，如果是一个富有的人做出同样的决定，那他就不需要在任何方面削减开支。

一些人如果收入越高，那么他们花费的也就越多——主要都是花费在所谓的常规商品上，如食物、度假和娱乐。但他们通常很少会买所谓的低档商品，公共交通就是一个例子。这些人不会去乘坐公交车，而是自己开车。

慈善家

一些富人不仅仅会把钱花在自己身上，他们也会向慈善机构捐出数以百万计的款项，或者以各种其他理由支持慈善事业。这些人通常被称为慈善家。"慈善"意味着帮助他人。

虚拟货币

在将来，你可能会完全抛弃今天所看到的硬币和纸币，在所有的交易中，你将代之以使用像信用卡或借记卡这样的塑料卡片。换句话说，货币将会实行电子化，或者，更进一步地，连这些塑料卡片都有可能消失。

那么，当钱看起来不再像钱的时候，钱又怎样才能成为钱呢？事实上，到那时，它看起来不像任何东西，因为你甚至都看不到它。你肯定不可能把它捡起来，也不可能把它放进你的钱包中。

电子货币就是那种在银行与银行之间、个人与个人之间进行转账并由电脑控制的钱。使用某些特殊的代码，计算机很容易就可以把钱从一个地方转移到另一个地方。

这种货币不一定是真实的，但它可以是虚拟的。

虚或实？

这种钱称为虚拟货币或虚拟钱币。"虚拟"指的是那些不以实物形式存在的你看不见、摸不着的东西,但是计算机软件却能够看得见、摸得着它。它虽不以实物形式存在,但是却与实际存在的事物非常接近。

你会信任这种虚拟货币吗?或许你并不信任,但虚拟货币的运作与真正的货币一样,越来越多的人已经开始使用它了。就像传统的钱一样,这些货币能够用来购买实物商品和服务。

比特币

在这类货币当中,比较流行的是比特币。比特币的制造和储存都实行了电子化。储存你的比特币的储钱罐实际上就是你的计算机。为了安全起见,比特币使用加密信息进行交易,因此它不可能被复制或被盗用。它不属于任何银行或任何其他机构,因此没有人能够干涉或控制它。

每个比特币都有一个代码,所以,如果你用它来买东西,便会有交易记录,之后,你就再也不能用这个比特币去购买其他任何东西了,因为它已经被用完了。因此,你在使用比特币进行消费时,其实就像是在使用真正的货币。

未来……

在你的有生之年，你可能会亲眼见证那些叮当作响的硬币以及纸币的终结。现在，实时处理全世界每个角落每一分每一秒都发生着的巨额交易的技术已经日趋成熟，很有可能在未来的10年内，钱让我们看到或感觉到的变化比过去6 000年内的变化还要大。

钱不断地被转账

今天，巨额资金以这种方式在世界各地转账。明天，也许我们在交易过程中使用的全都是电子货币。你的一生当中可能会使用这种货币数千次，但是可能你永远也看不到一分真正的钱。

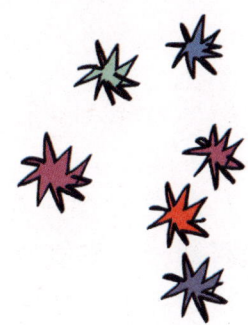

钱啊钱

所有这一切可能并不会对你造成太大的影响，除非你最终在金融公司工作。但是你还是必须赚钱、支付账单。你年纪越大，经你转手的钱就会越来越多，而且钱越多，你需要负的责任也就越大。

因此，你对有关钱的知识掌握得越多，你将来也就越能够更好地了解它和处理它……

……你也将能够更得心应手地控制你手中的钱。

讨 论

钱是长在树上的吗？

几乎每个人都希望钱是长在树上的。如果真是这样的话，那么生活可能会简单得多，同时我们的地球上也会拥有更多的森林。

但与我们的愿望相反的是，货币是有价值的，它可以用来交换同样具有价值的商品和服务。它是一种宝贵的东西。你花掉的每一分钱都必须是挣来的——通常是你父母每一个小时每一个小时辛苦工作挣来的工资。

你是怎么挣钱的？

如果你够幸运，那么你会得到一些补贴，这些补贴可以随便你花费。然而，许多父母认为，零花钱应该是孩子自己挣来的。你可以通过帮忙做家务活或做一些跑腿的工作而挣些零花钱。那么，你做哪些工作会帮到你的家庭呢？你可以问问你的邻居或家人或朋友，他们愿不愿意为家务活而支付给你工资。

什么样的购物习惯是不好的？

如果你真的需要买东西的话，那倒不算什么。但是，请不要为了娱乐而购物。请记住，家庭预算分为必需品和奢侈品两大类，因此，你需要明智地消费。最好的办法是，养成列清单的习惯，然后一直保持下去。你能想出其他让你控制自己消费的办法吗？

为什么你需要一个银行账号？

银行账号对你的父母亲来说是必不可少的，因为有了它，他们就可以把自己的钱安全地存放起来，而且还可以利用它支付账单。你可能有自己的储钱罐，那里存放着你的补贴和多余的零花钱，你也可以把钱存到银行里去。

如果你每周或每个月都存一点钱到银行里，之后银行会支付给你利息吗？讨论一下，你如何才能开立一个银行账户，以及想用你存下来的钱购买什么东西。

为什么你需要做好预算？

或许你已经发现，你所拥有的钱根本无法买到你所想要的每样东西，那些昂贵的物品对你来说是遥不可及的。但是，储蓄会让你的钱越来越多。如果你知道你为什么要储蓄，储蓄会给你带来什么好处，那你存钱的速度就会更快。

你为什么不创建一个愿望清单，以便知道需要在自己的账户里存够多少钱？你甚至可以给自己一个挣钱的期限，在某个日期之前存够钱。

中英文术语对照表

allowance
请参见 pocket money（零花钱）。

bank account 银行账户
同意银行照管钱的个人协议。

bitcoin 比特币
一种实验性的货币，它仅仅存在于电脑里，用于互联网上购买和销售商品之用。

budget 预算
同意花费的金额。

charity 慈善机构
以各种方式为处于困难中的人们提供帮助的组织。

consumer 消费者
定期购买商品的人，他们的购买行为是能够被预测的。

credit 信贷
借来的钱。

credit card 信用卡
能够让人们用借来的钱购买东西的卡。

currency 货币
以纸币或硬币的形式表示的钱，可用于买卖。

debit 借方
当有人需要支付时，从银行里取出来的金额。

debt 债务
需要偿还的借款。

depreciation 贬值
随着时间的推移，商品的价值越来越低。

donation 捐款
捐出的钱，通常捐给慈善机构。

electronic money 电子货币
并不是真正的钱，但是确实存在，只有计算机用户才能使用。

income 收入
通过工作赚得的钱。

Interest 利息
由于出借或投资而增加的钱，是按本金的一定百分比计算的。

loan 贷款
借给某人的一定数额的钱，但必须归还。

money cycle 货币周期
货币在商品买卖中周而复始流通的过程。

net worth 净值
个人所拥有的金钱和有价值的物品的总价值。

peer pressure 同龄人压力
指同龄人互相影响彼此待人处事的方式所产生的心理压力。

pester power 儿童消费力
儿童影响他们的父母亲为他们购买消费品的能力。

pocket money 零花钱
父母给孩子的并让孩子用于个人消费的钱。

point of purchase 购买点
指商店中的一个特殊的地方,在那里醒目地陈列着商品。

price 价格
购买东西的成本。

profit 利润
卖方由于定出了比成本更高的价格所获得的差额。

shopaholic 购物狂
指那些大量购物而且需要通过购买才会感到快乐的人。

spending power 消费能力
指某些特殊群体花钱的能力。

statistics 统计
收集人们具体做了什么的数字。

virtual money 虚拟货币
只存在于计算机中,但是已经被大众所认同的货币,它与真正的货币一样。

warranty 保证
卖方在销售商品时所出具的保证书,它承诺卖方所出售的商品都是正品,如果物品有损坏,将会得到维修。

索 引

account 账户 6, 10, 11, 20, 24, 25, 27, 55, 59, 60, 62
advertisement 广告 28, 28, 34, 36, 37, 46, 62
allowance 零花钱 12, 13, 14, 16, 46, 58, 59, 60, 62
ATM (Automated Teller Machine) 自动取款机 24
bank 银行 4, 6, 8, 9, 10, 11, 12, 19, 20, 21, 22, 23, 24, 25, 27, 42, 55, 59, 60, 62
bank account 银行账户 6, 11, 24, 25, 55, 59, 60, 62
banknote 钞票 4
bankrupt 破产 34
bargain 讨价还价，便宜货 34
bitcoin 比特币 55
borrowing 借钱 29, 40, 41, 42, 43
budget 预算 3, 12, 40, 44, 45, 58, 59, 60, 62
charity 慈善 19, 35, 49, 50, 51, 53
charity shop 慈善商店 35
clearance stock 清理库存，清仓 34
coin 硬币 4, 6, 8, 19, 54, 55, 59
compound interest 复利 27
consumer 消费者 9, 36, 39
contract 合同 14, 15
convenience store 便利店 31

credit 信贷，信用 4, 42, 43, 45, 55, 60, 62
credit card 信用卡 4, 42, 45, 60, 62
currency 货币 4
current account 活期账户 25
debit 借方 4, 24, 55
debt 债务 2, 40, 41, 42, 43, 60, 62
bebt collector 追债者 42
deposit 存款，存钱 24, 25
depreciate 贬值，降价 26
donation 捐赠 51
earning 收入 6,17
electronic money 电子货币 4, 55
foundation 基础 50
gold 黄金 4
goods 商品，货物 8, 26, 30, 32, 33, 38, 53, 58, 60
grant 补助 6
happiness 幸福 3, 52
homelessness 无家可归 49
income 收入 12, 50, 53, 60, 61, 62
inherit 继承 11
interest 利息 19, 20, 24, 25, 27, 40, 41, 43, 48, 59, 60, 62, 63
internet 互联网 25, 62
invest 投资 7, 9, 22, 24, 34
investments 投资 25, 27
job 工作（可数名词，侧重具体职业）

9, 15, 16, 58, 62
 legal age 法定年龄 24
 lending 出借 27, 40, 55
 loan 贷款 11, 40, 41, 63
 money cycle 货币周期 9
 money management 理财 9
 net worth 净值 11
 note 纸币 4, 6, 54
 online account 在线账户 25
 outlet stores 专卖店,直销店 35
 overseas aid 海外援助 48
 peer pressure 同龄压力 37
 pester power 儿童消费力 17
 philanthropy 慈善,慈善事业 53
 piggy bank 储钱罐 6, 19, 20, 22, 24, 59
 pocket money 零花钱 6, 13, 14, 16, 21, 42, 47, 58, 60, 63
 point of purchase 购买地点 33
 post office 邮局 20
 poverty 贫困,贫穷 49, 60, 63
 price 价格 26, 31
 product 产品 31, 32, 33, 34, 35
 profit 利润 20, 27
 pygg 储钱罐 23
 ration book (定量)购物证 38
 refugee 难民 48
 refund 退款 35
 repayment 还款 41, 43
 sale 销售 34
 saving 储蓄 4, 6, 10, 11, 18, 20, 21, 22, 24, 25, 27, 44, 59
 savings account 储蓄账户 10
 savings bonds 储蓄债券 11

shop 商店 2, 8, 31, 32, 33, 34, 35, 38, 58, 63
shopaholic 购物狂 39
shopping 购物 28, 31, 32, 33, 35, 58
shop 商店 2, 8, 31, 32, 33, 34, 35, 38, 58, 63
simple interest 单利 27, 63
spending 支出,消费 2, 3, 6, 7, 9, 12, 13, 17, 18, 19, 20, 21, 26, 28, 29, 30, 31, 33, 34, 36, 37, 43, 44, 46, 47, 53, 58
spending power 消费能力 36, 46
statement 声明 25, 60
statistics 统计 3, 46
stock 股票 31, 34, 35
store 商店 31, 32, 33, 35
street vendor 街边小摊 34
tax 税收 50, 60, 61, 62, 63
trust money 信托资金 11
tween 青少年 46
value 价值 5, 13, 20, 26, 28, 58
virtual money 虚拟货币 55
warranty 保证 34
wealth 财富 3, 52
will 意愿,意志 11
work 工作（不可数名词，侧重体力或脑力劳动）6, 9, 14, 16, 22, 31, 48, 58, 60, 61, 63

63

译后记

近年来，金融素养已成为培养孩子全面发展的一个重要方面。早在20世纪30年代，美国就开始了对中小学生进行与生活密切相关的理财教育。如今，美国中小学理财教育日趋成熟，主要围绕让中小学生正确地"认识钱、花钱、挣钱、借钱、分享钱以及让钱增值"而展开。在英国，随着金融理财教育的需求不断上升，金融监管局将个人理财知识纳入2008年实施的《国民教育教学大纲（修订）》中，要求中小学校必须对毕业生进行良好的金融知识教育。我国周边的国家如孟加拉、斯里兰卡等，也早已开设了此类课程。

中国的孩子也同样对生活中的金融知识充满渴求。2014年春节期间，《新京报》记者调查了北京90名10~13岁的孩子，结果发现，孩子们平均收到了4 867元压岁钱，比前一年上涨了5%，其中收得最多的孩子，压岁钱有2万元，而一半以上的孩子收到的压岁钱在1 000~5 000元之间。孩子们的压岁钱该怎么处理？一部分家长的做法是直接"据为己有"：要么存入自己的银行账户，要么用到家庭的日常开支及急需的事情上。虽然也有些家长孩子的主体意识和理财意识比较强，但多局限于将孩子的压岁钱存入银行、做定投基金和购买保险等方面。其实，多数孩子都渴望由自己来管理这笔数额不少的钱，但苦于没有一定的金融和理财知识，除了交给父母或买点零食、添加一些课辅用品等之外，也不知道怎么办。因此，及时地向他们普及金融知识，让他们学会理财，应该是时候了。

华夏出版社从英国引进的"华夏少儿金融智慧屋——货币系列"丛书（共4册，中英双语）确实是应时应景之作，它涉及四个主题——世界货币、国家货币、家庭理财和个人理财，它们相互补充，构成一个整体，以孩子们喜爱的绘本形式，把晦涩难懂的国际金融、货币、贸易、经济知识转化为生动有趣的语言，用最浅显的语言全面地阐述了"金融的逻辑"，让孩子们在轻松愉悦的阅读过程中全面触摸金融知识。

完成这一系列书，我要特别感谢我的儿子贾岚晴，这套书献给已是小学生的他。我还要感谢我的先生贾拥民，感谢他一直以来对我的支持、鼓励和帮助。感谢我的母亲蒋仁娟、父亲傅美峰对我儿子的悉心照顾，使我得以安心从事翻译工作。我的朋友和同事傅晓燕、鲍玮玮、傅锐飞、傅旭飞、陈贞芳、郑文英等，也给予了我很多支持和帮助，在此一并致以诚挚的谢意！

感谢华夏出版社一直以来对我的信任！

傅瑞蓉
2015年11月于杭州

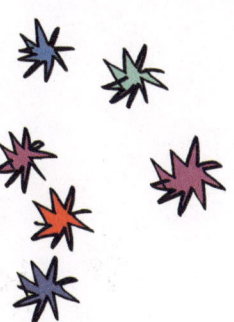

附　英文影印版

小·贴士

小朋友,为了方便中英文对照阅读,我们排版时尽可能使中文和英文页码一一对应,但由于中英文表达习惯不同,有个别页码的尾行可能会出现不对应的情况,这时,你只要往后翻一页就会找到哦。——编者

Contents

4-5 **What is money?**
Is money just the stuff jingling in your pocket or purse – or more?

6-7 **Money is a must**
You can do lots of different things with money – just keep it on the move!

8-9 **Money goes round**
When you pay for something in a shop, the cash doesn't sit in the till for long.

10-17 **Receiving money**
Hurray! There's some money coming your way.

18-19 **Three choices**
You can spend your cash, save it or give it away. You have three choices.

20-27 **Save it!**
The best way to save is to give your money to someone else to make it grow!

28-37 **Spend it!**
How to spend wisely on the things you need and not to waste your precious cash.

38-39 **What a waste!**
Buying things you don't need often results from listening to other people.

40-43 **Borrowing and debt**
Getting into debt, even if you are borrowing from family or close friends, can cause problems.

44-45 **Budgeting**
You can manage your money much more easily if you draw up a budget.

46-47 **What statistics?**
Statistics tell people all about you and your money and how you spend it.

48-51 **Give it away!**
You can help people all over the world by giving away a little of your cash.

52-53 **Rich and poor**
Does wealth really bring happiness, or does it lead to a life of frustration?

54-55 **Virtual money**
Is money really money when it doesn't exist?

56-57 **For the future...**
What next?

58-59 **Let's discuss**
Money does'nt grow on trees
earning, spending, saving, budgeting

60-61 **Glossary**

62-63 **Index**

What is money?

The obvious answer to this question is that money is the stuff jingling in your pocket or purse, as well as the banknotes that seem to vanish as quickly as you get them. But if the coins and notes were from another country and couldn't buy you as much as a bus ticket at home, would you still call them money? And what about plastic money – debit and credit cards?

Money promises

Of course, you'd rather have the coins and notes anytime. The notes may be bits of paper that promise 'to act as money' but they are by far the most popular form of money. Then there's credit cards and gold – that's money isn't it? There's even a form of money that you can't see or touch – electronic money. Is all this really money?

Money goes out

It doesn't take much to see that money is still changing its shape and form. Also, money isn't being used in the same way everywhere. This is mainly because money isn't just about currency – coins and notes, or even credit cards. It's about banks and savings, about money that flows around the world.

6,000 Years of Money!

As we find out just what is and what isn't seen as money today, we'll discover that all sorts of crazy forms of money have cropped up in the past – amber, beads, cowrie shells, drums, eggs, feathers, to name but a few.

In fact, you could use anything as money – even a few sheep – as long as everyone agreed on their value.

Money has been around in one form or another for 6,000 years! The fact is that money wasn't just invented in one place. It developed in all kinds of ways and in many different parts of the world.

But no matter what object was used as money, it always had 4 qualities:
* Everyone agreed to use it.
* Everyone agreed that it could be used in different ways.
* Everyone agreed that it had a value which might change but which everyone would accept.
* Everyone agreed to respect what it stood for.

So let's find out how money works for you.

Money is a must

Do you have money? Do you have money jingling in your pocket today? A purse full of coins and notes in your wallet? Or a piggy bank where you pop all those spare coins? Even a savings or bank account of your own?

you have money!

If you have any of these, you have money! And it's likely that you'll have more and more money as the months and years go by.

in and out

Money is like water – it flows freely – in and out of everyone's pockets. It will definitely flow in and out of your pocket for the whole of your life, but will it flow out faster than it flows in?

If it flows in, you're earning. You may have to work for the money, or you may be given it as pocket money, a gift or a grant. If it flows out, you're spending. You're buying things and paying for them. If it flows in faster than it flows out, you'll be rich. If it doesn't, you'll have problems.

Money's Fun too!

Earning it is fun and spending it is definitely fun! But you can do better than this. You can 'grow' your money, or invest it. Now that's a real challenge!

And you can spend it in special ways. You can spend it so that you earn from it at the same time. That's an even bigger challenge!

Or you can share it. You can share it with people who will be helped in a really big way. Imagine being able to help someone like that!

* We think about it and talk about it.
* We love having it and couldn't buy much without it.
* We need it for necessities like food and shelter.
* We enjoy it for the fun things

So money is a 'must'. It's something you can't escape from, but this doesn't have to be a bad thing. Just the opposite – it's something you can take control of, have fun with, grow, spend, and help people with.

And it's never too early to start!

Money goes round

1
You pocket the packet of gum and put your coins on the counter.

6
The change falls into a child's hand. In half an hour, it's being handed over the counter of the local sweet shop.

Spending puts your money into circulation

You pass money across a counter for goods. The shopkeeper passes it to the bank who passes it to people – and so on, and so on.

2
Money goes round and round.

3
The coins find themselves in and out of another four tills that same day.

5
The bank holds them just two days before they're delivered to the owner of an amusement arcade to be given out as change.

4
At the weekend, they're bagged and delivered to the bank.

The Facts!

✳ The role of young people in moving money around is growing, and this involves YOU.

✳ You're not just a buyer, a consumer, you're already an important part of the money cycle.

✳ Young people have never had so much money, and spending isn't the only thing you can do with it! It's time for you to get started on money management.

✳ Jobs for young people are set to change. There'll be less stable work on offer but more openings to go it alone, and more power and more help and responsibility to call on.

✳ You're young. You may be inexperienced but you have assets to sell – you can be polite, punctual, bright, responsible, honest, and people will invest in you for these reasons.

The future is all before you. You are probably more money-wise than your parents were at your age – and the opportunities before you are also far greater.

Receiving money

It's always great when you're surprised with a gift of money. You might get a small thrill from finding a coin in the gutter or from unearthing a shoebox of cash on a rubbish dump. Odds are that both these things won't come your way! But (surprise! surprise!) there might be a stash of cash with your name on it right now, or coming your way sometime in the future, that could change your life.

Birthday money

You may have been given money for your birthday by fond relatives – perhaps you even received money when you were born, in which case your parents may have already opened a bank or savings account in your name. Could your parents have been putting money away into an account for years and have forgotten to tell you about it?

Trust money

Your parents may even have established a trust fund for you. Sometimes grown-ups set up trust funds at a bank, or put money in a loan or savings account where it's invested until such time as a child is old enough to have access to it for themselves. Usually, an age is established before which the funds cannot be touched.

Inheriting money

A sad way to get money is to inherit it when a person dies. A will is a legal document that says how a person's assets will be shared out after their death. If no will exists, a dead person is said to be intestate and laws have to be used to decide the list of heirs. You might still inherit, but a stranger might have decided just what you get!

Your assets

It goes without saying that if any of these windfalls drop into your lap, they should be used wisely. If you have money in savings bonds, or trust funds, or bank accounts, or anything else, you have what's called assets. And assets establish your financial value, known as your net worth. The older you get, the more important your net worth will be. It may get you financial help from the bank to buy your dream purchase, to help you through college or to fund that round-the-world student trip.

Pocket money

A regular income

Pocket money is your first step to receiving a regular income. It can be relied on to come in each week, more or less on time, and in full. You can 'bank on it' as they say, which also means you can be planning how you're going to spend it long before it arrives.

You may like to agree a weekly or monthly allowance depending on how the family budget is arranged. It will also depend on how far you can trust yourself to stick to a financial plan, known as a budget. It's no good taking a monthly sum if you can't trust yourself not to blow it all in the first week!

Are you getting an allowance?

There are different opinions about the value of giving allowances or pocket money to young people, and you may find your parents need a little persuasion. You may have parents who already know all of this – they believe it's important for you to start handling your own money at a young age.

How much?

How much pocket money you get depends on how much money your parents have available to give you or how much they think you should have.

Bearing in mind that parents want the best for you, accept pocket money as you would accept a gift. After all, that's what it really is. Even if it's a small amount, it's worth establishing that you're grateful.

MEMO TO PARENTS

* Having pocket money is good for your child.
* It encourages a sense of independence.
* It helps kids understand the value of money.
* It teaches them to take decisions on whether to spend it all straight away, or save for a few weeks so they can buy something special.

Ages and stages

Increase pocket money by a fixed amount on each birthday. If your child is old enough to help out with household chores, arrange top-ups to pocket money in exchange for more involvement around the home.

Those chores!

Your parents may give you a weekly allowance in return for you taking responsibility for certain chores around the house. It's unlikely you'll grow up in a world where wads of cash continue to come your way free of responsibilities, so this is good practice for the future.

Strings attached!

So – with pocket money comes responsibility. If pocket money has strings attached which require you to carry out certain chores, it's worth making an agreement, a contract, with your parents which details EXACTLY what they expect of you.

Small jobs make a difference

Chores may be simply helping around the kitchen or involve just keeping your own room clean – which you should be doing anyway! They may involve care of pets, washing the car or work in the garden.

They'll certainly help your parents out and involve you in taking on some of the workload of the entire household.

it's in the contract

Why is it important to have this 'contract' decided up front? Once you've agreed what you get paid for, and what you don't, your parents will expect you to stick to this. Expect trouble when you don't live up to expectations – you forget to make your bed, switch off the lights downstairs, or put the cat out.

A few useful chores can cement the pocket money contract at home.

Tit for tat

There are, of course, parents who think that helping with the household chores should be part of your involvement anyway and aren't happy about having to pay you for this.

JOBS YOU CAN DO

Garage cleaner
Painter of garden furniture /fences
Gardener
Car washer
Snow shoveller
Cleaning, window cleaning
Riding school helper
Plant sitter

Party entertainer: clown, magician, balloon modeller, storyteller, actor, musician
Animals' shelter worker: clean kennels, walk dogs, feed animals
Pet sitter
Adopt a granny/grandpa

Deliveries
Computer design: making cards, signs etc.
Plant sales: grow herbs in small pots
Selling old clothes, toys, games
T-shirt design

Earning money

It isn't long before you begin to understand that the most reliable way of getting hold of money is to earn it. Your pocket money or allowance may already come with strings attached – the odd household chore for a buck or two. But joining the labour market – selling your time, effort and expertise outside the home – not only brings in the cash but gets you a lot more benefits as well.

first job

Your first job will almost certainly be running alongside schoolwork. Don't underestimate the demands. If you take on work, you will need to be committed to it for the time it takes. Work will need to be a priority just like school is.

Added to this, you'll not want to give up your sports activities or your social or family life. So fitting it all in will take extra doses of energy and organisation. Make sure you've thought this all out before you take the leap.

Regular work can be taken on to earn extra allowances.

Reward for Effort

Finally, you'll be earning money that rewards your effort and contribution – that should make you feel good! You should get a real sense of personal accomplishment and a confidence boost!

PESTER POWER

Young people exercise enormous control over family spending through 'pester power', the power to persuade parents to spend money. More than two thirds of teens say they have the power to influence their parents' buying decisions.
And they twist them round their little fingers ...

Researchers have repeatedly found that parents hate saying 'no' to teens. They're more likely to go without something themselves than deny their children.

Three choices

Money is just a piece of metal or paper – or a plastic card – until you use it to make something happen. You can use it in just 3 different ways – you either spend it, save it or give it away. Any one of these will bring different results.

Spend it!

For those who like to spend, money is the best thing that ever happened. It's the key to hours of shopping and owning things – new things. It can be the trigger to a bad habit – to shopping for shopping's sake!

It can also be the entry to new experiences and adventures, helping you to join clubs and make contacts who share your interests. If you have spent your money wisely, then you have the benefit of all those new possessions or experiences.

Save it!

It's amazing how some people can save money easily. It seems to come naturally to them. People can be as different about the way they handle money as they are in the way they look, or the things they're interested in.

You save money by simply not spending the money you earn or are given. If it's just a few coins, you can save it in a piggy bank. But when you get more, you may want to put it in a bank which will give you a little extra, called interest, each month.

Give it away!

Sharing is something you usually do because you want to, not because you have to. Handouts to friends are probably done knowing your friends will return the favour sometime. But it feels good to actually help someone who desperately needs it. There are plenty of people in this situation. Dropping a few coins into a charity box each week means that someone somewhere will be helped by YOU. And you could get directly involved and actually see how your contribution is helping.

Save it!

For many people, saving isn't nearly as easy as spending. Some even talk about saving as if it's the opposite of spending. Perhaps it feels that way – but it's NOT! You could say that instead of losing £10 out of your pocket, you have gained £10 by holding on to it. But is it really that simple?

Sleeping cash

If, to you, saving means stashing all your cash in your mattress and letting it lie there, then you could find the value of your 'stash' goes down in time. And if you pop it into your piggy bank, then it will sit there doing nothing just the same. So this is not the kind of saving you want to be doing.

Working cash

Instead, there are ways of saving, which, just like spending, involve putting your money into circulation. When you put your money into a savings account at the bank or post office, you are trusting someone else to make it grow. The bank invests it in business deals and it tries to earn a profit, and some of that profit is given back to you as interest.

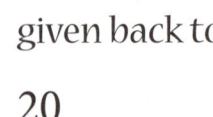

WHAT KIND OF SAVER ARE YOU?

The NON-saver
* You spend without thinking about what you need or what you want.
* You don't do without the odd luxury and save nothing.
* Your money often runs out before more comes in.

The small saver
* You spend but you weigh up what you need and what you want.
* Maybe you do without the odd luxury so you can save a bit.
* The money you save begins to add up.
* And the more you have, the better you feel about it.
* You can still buy a few things when you want to.
* You can deal with emergencies.
* You can buy things that you couldn't afford with just a week's, or a month's, pocket money.
* You're learning life skills.

The BIG saver
* You spend as little as possible.
* You'd rather save money, so spend only on necessities.
* You put as much as you can into the bank.

Piggy banks

Most kids have owned a piggy bank at some time or another. But why a piggy bank? Why not a rhinoceros bank or an aardvark bank? Are pigs thought to be better than other animals at saving their hard-earned cash? Well – maybe, but that's not why we have piggy banks.

Fattening up!

In earlier times, in Western societies, a pig was a kind of poor man's money box. A piglet, bought from the market in spring, could live on household leftovers and would be fattened up and ready for the butcher just before the winter. Your piggy bank, which is fed on leftovers of your money, fattens in the same way, and can be smashed to pieces when it's full.

In German-speaking countries it was the custom to give apprentices – young people who were training to become craftsmen – a pig as reward for a year's work. The pig, therefore, became the symbol of investing – both with money and in young people!

pyggs

Many years ago, people kept pots and jugs in their kitchen made from a kind of clay called pygg. When they wanted to put some money away, they'd put it in these pots or jars for safety. In time, the receptacles became known as pygg banks, then pyggy banks.

No doubt it didn't take long for someone to come up with the idea of a pygg bank actually shaped like a pig. And so the piggy bank was born.

Traditional clay pyggs looked like this.

The piggy bank we know today.

Money in the bank

So you have some money and you've decided against the piggy bank and the mattress. But is it enough money to open a bank account? A bank will normally expect you to keep a minimum amount of money in your new account, enough to make it worth their while. If you dip below this amount, you may get charged a fine, so this is the first thing to find out.

What's in it for you?

The bank may require a minimum deposit.

In exchange you get:
* somewhere to place your cash
* somewhere to invest your cash
* a savings account with interest paid on the balance. (See pages 26 and 27 to find out about interest.)
* a debit card so you can withdraw cash from the ATM (Automatic Teller Machine) and pay by card in shops
* and even, maybe, a free gift or two. Banks are always looking for new young customers.

Old enough?

The BIG issue is age. If you want a bank account of your own, you will have to be 18 years old, or legal age, in many countries. But don't give up. Your parents can help you get your own account opened. This doesn't mean that it belongs to your parents – you will still get privacy and your mail sent to you.

BANK ACCOUNTS

Online account
Your bank will almost certainly be able to set you up with internet access to your account so you can find out at any time what is happening to your balance – and your investments.

Current account
All banks will offer you a current account – one that allows you to place, or deposit, money, and withdraw it whenever you like. You won't get any interest on this because the amount may go up and down on the hour. However, some banks do pay interest on current accounts if the balance hits a certain spot – so it's best to ask. You should arrange to have a statement sent to you each month or you can check it online.

Savings account
To make sure that you are 'growing' your money, you need to set up a savings account. There are various kinds on offer, dependent upon how much money you want to place and for how long. Obviously, the longer the bank can be
certain that it has your cash, the better the deal it will offer you.

Growing money

One of the great things about money is that it doesn't lose value in itself. If you hide £5 under the mattress, you'll still have £5 when you go to find it later. It may not buy you as much, but it'll still be £5.

When you spend money on goods, things change. Goods depreciate. What does 'depreciate' mean? It means that over time, the value you paid for something starts to decrease. The older most things get, the less they are worth.

In some ways, money and goods behave in the same way. The goods get older and are worth less. The money stays the same, but the world outside changes. Rising prices make your money buy less – so it's worth less.

The only way to combat all this is to make your money grow.

EARNING INTEREST

When you put your money in your savings account at the bank, you expect your money to grow. This happens because the bank uses your money in its business investments and it will pay you a fee for this use. The fee is known as interest.

Interest is the profit or reward paid to the lender. Interest is interesting because anyone can do it and make their money grow a little – or sometimes a lot.

You can earn interest either as simple interest or compound interest.

Simple interest just keeps adding interest to your original amount. This is how it grows if your £1 earns interest at 10% for 5 years.

Year	Total investment	Interest rate	Simple interest
1	£1	10% per annum	£1.10
2			£1.20
3			£1.30
4			£1.40
5			£1.50

Compound interest pays better than simple interest. The interest may be the same, and the time the same, but now the interest is added to the total savings AND the interest it has earned. It grows your money much faster.

Year	Total investment	Interest rate	Compound interest
1	£1	10% per annum	£1.10
2			£1.21
3			£1.33
4			£1.46
5			£1.61

Spend it!

We all love spending money. It gives us the things we want, it makes us feel good – and it's not that difficult! There's no shortage of things to spend your money on. But just in case you run out of ideas, you're bombarded with ads in the street, in magazines, on TV, and – when you've actually bought something – even on your shopping bags.

Wise spending

But spending money brings a certain responsibility. You can only spend the money you have. If you're careful with your spending, everything's fine. If you're reckless, you can end up in trouble.

The Value of Money

When grown-ups lecture you about understanding the value of money, it's really this that they're talking about – knowing how to spend wisely.

WHAT KIND OF SPENDER ARE YOU?

The NON-spender
* You hoard every penny that comes your way.
* You do without – or 'make do' – rather than use your precious cash to buy things.
* The money you don't spend begins to add up.

The CAREFUL spender
* You spend but you weigh up what you need and what you want.
* Maybe you do without the odd luxury so you can save a bit.
* The money you save begins to add up.

The BIG spender
* You spend and spend and blow all your money.
* You feel good, you look good, you've got loads of stuff.
* You look 'big' and successful to your friends.
* You've got 'power in your pocket' – for the moment.
* And when it's all gone, you come down with a bump.
* You've never got anything put by for emergencies.
* You've never got enough for the fantastic thing you've always wanted but just can't afford.
* You overstretch your spending and sometimes have to borrow.

Shops

Most spending takes place in shops. Today, they are often modern, glitzy places full of excitement and appealing goods. But this is a fairly new development.

Shops develop

Shops have come a long way since the earliest days when pedlars used to walk the streets of cities and country roads, selling their wares from a small horse and cart or even from a simple tray.

And even when shops started to open in the main street, they would be pretty limited – a butcher, a baker and a candlestick maker.

Your grandparents, maybe their parents, will remember a time when there were few clothing shops, no music shops selling discs and records, and certainly no electric shops selling steam irons and TVs.

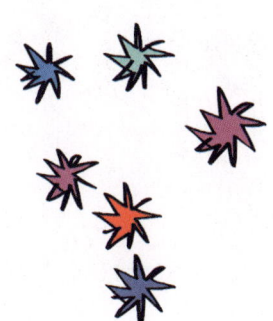 

Stock it!

Do you expect to buy goldfish food in the grocers? A hair slide in the paper shop? A newspaper at the garage? Seems odd but it's what happens. More and more, shops limit their stock to the most frequently requested items.

A single shop can sell a whole range of items. Some are old-fashioned 'corner shops' that stock everything the local community could possibly need. Some, like petrol stations, know that once you've stopped your car and got out of it, you want to get the shopping done as quickly as possible.

Convenience shopping, as it's called, is the new way forward. People work longer and longer hours and have less and less time to shop. And whether you're a local or a stranger in town, convenience stores always look and feel the same and carry much the same stock.

Price

Price is important. People have a limited amount of money to spend, and if they spend more on one thing, they cannot spend it on another.

When the price of a product goes up, other competitive and cheaper products will sell better. People will buy more hamburgers if the price is £1.00 per kilo than if it is £2.00.

Going shopping

Which are your favourite shops and stores? You'll certainly have some. One of the most surprising things about our shopping habits, is that we tend to visit a few favourite stores over and over again and rarely change our shopping pattern. We like the way they're laid out, the goods they carry, or the staff perhaps!

We like the fact that when we visit them, everything is exactly as we would expect to find it. There are no surprises. We feel comfortable. And the store planners know this so they limit any change they make so you continue to feel at home.

Atmosphere

The layout of stores varies enormously, from the shop piled high with boxes and goods, to the simplicity of a mobile phone shop with low lighting and shiny steel. Whatever the decor, it is planned to create the best atmosphere to make you buy.

Lifestyle

If the store is selling a lifestyle product, it may have wider, more spacious aisles, cool colours, just a few carefully chosen items placed at eye level – even a seat or two and soft music playing. It makes you feel expensive.

Familiarity

We each have just a few favourite shops where we buy. We tread the same route down the street, passing some shops and entering others. Even a new store opening rarely changes our pattern. We know what we like!

POP!

POP is shop speak for the point of purchase, sometimes called the point of sale – the place where you meet the product! In a shop, this is the rack or shelf where the product is laid out. But is it all laid out at random on the off-chance that you might stop and pick it up? It's not!

The shopkeeper knows that up to three quarters of all purchases are made by customers who are pottering round the store. They spend only ten seconds looking at any one rack or shelf. So the goods must all be displayed at the right level – within eyeshot and easy reach. They must be packaged to catch your eye.

But there must be entertainment as well. Free-standing displays mean you have to walk round or behind the product, perhaps look up or peep under. It's a game of hide-and-seek designed to keep you interested, to keep you guessing.

To make shopping fun!

Displays offer lots of choice to hold your attention in the store.

We shop at the same stores over and over again.

An uncluttered window display attracts sophisticated buyers.

Bargains

We all love a bargain. Nothing feels quite as good as buying something 'on the cheap'. Finding a bargain isn't difficult if you spend time hunting from shop to shop for the item that's a bit cheaper, or for the one marked down or on special offer.

Street vendors often specialise in one kind of product.

There are plenty of places to find them!

Street Vendors

Street vendors stand on the street corner and appear to sell the very same things as the shops – except they're far cheaper. But remember, if you want to return the product for any reason, the street vendor may not be there the next day. Apart from this risk, street vendors offer good deals, selling clearance stock or stock from a company that has closed down.

Bankrupt Stock

Sales advertising bankrupt stock are often genuine sales arising from the closure of a company. There will be good bargains to pick up, but remember to check that you still get a warranty, a guarantee that things will be mended or exchanged if they go wrong. And invest in some extra spare parts if they're available, since the manufacturer won't be there to replace breakages.

Buying online

Buying online should be cheaper. After all, there are no store costs to add to the price, no big buildings, no salespeople. But photos can make things look better than they are, colours don't match what you saw or the fabric is a disappointment. However, you can return what you don't want. Remember to unwrap all products carefully – you'll need to repackage them exactly as they came if you want your refund in full. And always keep a record of returns.

Outlet stores

Outlet stores are a recent arrival on the bargain shopping scene. Designers and manufacturers of every kind of product change their designs and stock each year – sometimes more than once. The old stuff must go to make way for the new. Outlet stores often specialise in designer labels and seasonal fashions, so even if you're one season behind, you can still wear that smart label.

Charity shops

Charity shops are full of bargains. They only sell the best of the stuff given to them and it's all likely to be there. And you are doing some good when you buy. Every charity shop is run to raise funds for a cause, and you're helping them in their efforts with every small purchase.

Pressure to buy

As you get older, there's increased pressure from all kinds of companies that want you to buy their stuff – and from some of your friends who've already got it! Manufacturers need to **advertise** to inform consumers about products. But it's also about persuading them to buy. It's about making you think you need something when maybe you don't.

Part of the Crowd

Advertisers think you're fickle. They think you show no loyalty to any brand and will shift your spending to whatever is cool or most fashionable at the time. They use clever techniques, and almost all ads are based on one of them. There's the ad that tells you if you don't buy you're going to feel left out, not 'part of the crowd'. Everyone else is right or knows something you don't.

But be an individual! Buy the things you want, however 'different' and 'strange' they may be. Recognise advertising for what it is ...

... and make your own choices!

Peer Pressure

There's nothing easy about resisting peer pressure. The need to fit in stays with us for most of our lives. Copying classmates and friends, aspiring to magazine pictures of the trendy, judging yourself by what others say about you, is all part of this pattern. You have to be pretty gutsy to stand out from the crowd and do your own thing.

Be Yourself!

But doing what is best for YOU, wearing what suits YOU, and expressing your own opinions, is part of being YOU and not a copycat of everybody else.

Remember that manufacturers, retailers and advertisers worldwide are relying on you to do what everybody else does. They make money by creating mass fashions, mass attitudes and mass buying fads.

Being one of the crowd is comfortable – but don't let your peers influence you too much.

Getting to You

Advertisers are spending billions of dollars a year to target your purse, and you're watching thousands of their advertisements a year. That's a lot of pressure! The average young person will have received 250,000 **media messages** involving advertising by the time they're 15.

What a waste!

How many pairs of jeans have you got in your wardrobe? How many T-shirts, blouses or other unworn clothes are there that have never been taken off the hanger? We buy for all kinds of reasons, but few are because we don't have something. It's more likely to be for a different reason – and not always one that makes a lot of sense.

Spoilt for choice

If you want a chocolate bar, you have twenty to choose from. Need a breakfast cereal? There are twelve kinds! A sweater – a hundred! A magazine? When it comes to food and clothing and entertainment, we're spoilt for choice.

Back in the good old days ...

There was a time when things like these were considered essentials. In fact, after the Second World War, you had to take your ration book to the shop to get your one permitted item. This was back in the 1950s, so someone in your family will remember it. It's not that long ago! But today, with goods pouring in from all over the world, there's more than enough for everyone – and no one has to queue for a pair of winter knickers.

Shopaholics!

Compared to the 'famous' days of rationing, there's no doubt that we've become spoilt. We're almost all shopaholics. We're wasteful, chucking things away because they're not new. We throw food away, not because it's gone off, but because we have a crisper, fresher version. We throw a shirt away because it would cost more to take it to the dry cleaner than to replace it.

Over-consuming

In many developed countries, people have become such expert consumers that they overbuy knowingly. And many throw away a large proportion of what they buy and think nothing of it. In the UK, it's been worked out that people throw away 30% of the food they buy. The truth is, we've become very wasteful.

Waste often ends up in huge unsightly tips like this one.

Borrowing and debt

However hard you try to manage your budget, there are always going to be times when you need that extra bit. One of the key problems with running out of money when you really need it, is that you have to ask someone to help. You have to find someone to LEND you money and you have to BORROW it on terms that are not too harsh.

From friends

Friends are more likely than anyone else to help you out with a loan – an interest-free loan! In other words, they'll lend you money to be repaid, pound for pound. Having said that, any loan is a debt. And debts have a nasty habit of turning sour.

While you owe money to a friend, you may get asked to help them out with odd favours and, of course, it's difficult to say 'no'.

Above all, remember that even if the loan is quite casual, it is a loan and not a gift. Friendships often fall apart when borrowers forget their obligations.

From Parents

Borrowing from your parents can be as casual as borrowing from a friend – but not always. Depending on the amount of the loan, you'll need to negotiate how much and how often you make repayments.

And bear in mind there'll be no further subs or loans or helping handouts if you get this wrong. Parents are great at telling you that you don't deserve a second chance, and they're right of course. If you've got the guts to borrow from them in the first place, you're certainly old enough to be taking responsibility for the repayments.

And parents might just charge interest – not necessarily in money terms, but they'll be bound to ask for those extra chores and courtesies whilst you're in their debt.

Debt and credit

It may seem odd to warn you about the dangers of debt when you're still just getting pocket money. But this isn't to advise you on the here and now so much as to make you aware of the consequences of what may happen later on.

See it coming

Too often people are plunged into more debt because they just didn't realise how difficult things might become once they were in debt. It doesn't help when credit card companies and banks put us under pressure to borrow. So, if you're aware right now of what happens when you get into debt, you might just think twice about drifting down that route in the future.

Can't pay

Debt doesn't become a problem until you're not able to pay it back. This is the bit that needs to be avoided at all costs, even if it does mean doing without things you want.

When things get truly bad, there are people known as debt collectors who are employed to come to your home and take back all the things you now can't pay for ... just imagine!

THE DIFFICULT STUFF

A debt is what you owe to someone or to a company when you borrow money from them.

The trick with debt is to only borrow what you can afford to pay back over a set period of time. If you don't have enough money to cover the repayments each month, don't take the debt out. It seems simple, but many people get it wrong – and it's not always their fault. Any debt is a risk, so you need to cut the risk to a minimum.

What is debt?
The consequences of being in debt can be pretty grim:
* You worry about it all the time.
* You can't spend what you want.
* All your spare money goes into paying off the charges or interest that's mounting on the debt.
* You can't see the end of it.

What is credit?
Credit is a loan of a fixed amount. It is how much a lender decides can be lent to you based on your financial value, your net worth. Like a loan, the credit amount can be spent by you and must be repaid. If the lender has got it right, the loan won't cause you too much hardship to repay. Of course, many companies get it wrong. Many borrowers are offered too much credit. And then the problems arise!

Budgeting

Working out a budget can begin as soon as you start getting pocket money.

Budgeting is the simplest form of money management. It's not the most exciting part. In fact, spending, and even saving, beat budgeting by a long shot! But it's one of those things that gets easier (once you've done it).

Budgeting is like going to the dentist. It's a tough call, but you know it's doing you good!

Can i afford it?

Making a budget means you recognise that your money supply is limited – and that's not fun! It almost certainly means that you want to do lots of things you know you may not be able to afford.

The good news is that once your budget is drawn up, it'll stop you worrying about whatever spending you're going to do, and that should make it all worthwhile!

Yes I can!

A budget will almost certainly show you that there IS enough money to do the things you want. You may have to save over time to achieve them, even wait a little. You may have to buy something in parts rather than straight off – your CD collection, for example, or your winter outfit!

No I can't

It's not always easy to put off doing something you want to do or buying something you think you need. We live in a world of promises. Get it now – pay later! Put it on a credit card! Worry about it when the bill turns up!

If you go along with this approach, you'll almost certainly suffer from bad budgeting habits. You may get someone to help you out because you're young or 'you don't know any better' – but unfortunately, this will change. In the real world, the only people who'll help you out may well want a lot of money to do so.

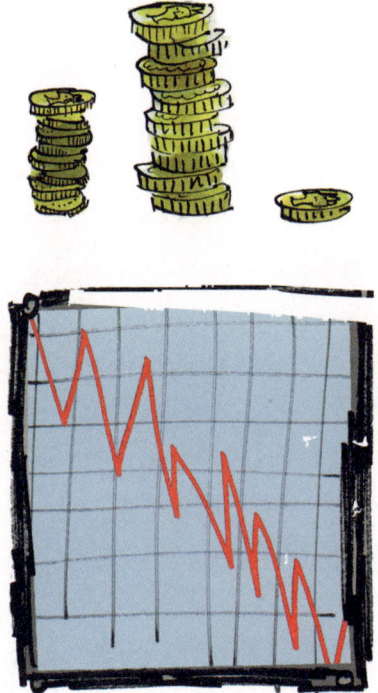

Above all, budgets require self-discipline.

What statistics?

Teens 'n tweens

Young teenagers – (13-15) are particularly savvy. They receive and spend more in an attempt to gain freedom from parents and from rules and routine. Life is focused on fun, fashion and friends.

The many million strong group known as 'tweens' – (8-12) have more spending power than ever before as working parents shower them with cash to ease their guilt.

✻ The average allowance is £8 per week.
✻ Tweens want to feel and look older, like their older siblings, and their taste is for more grown-up products.
✻ They love mobile phones.

A mobile world

Cell phones are a popular way to keep in touch with friends, play games and find the latest fashion accessory.

✻ The world now has over 1 billion mobile phones.
✻ 60% of young people in the UK (1 million) own a cell phone or have access to their parents' mobile.
✻ The average age for getting a cell phone is 14 years old.
✻ Text messaging is the top method of communicating for young people.

Advertising at you!

✻ Do you watch TV at certain times, early evening and Saturday morning?
✻ Do you think there's too much advertising targeted at you?
✻ Do you think there's too much sweet and fast food advertising targeted at you?

Well – you should!

Statisticians are watching you all the time – recording how much you're spending and where. This is because you spend so much! You make a real difference to the economy of the country you live in, so retailers and manufacturers want to know all about you.

Big spenders

Most (60%) of your spending money (£1,375 a year) comes from pocket money or allowances. The rest comes from doing chores, from gifts and from Saturday jobs.

✳ But who spends most? Girls or boys?
✳ Who saves most? Girls or boys?

The answers are girls each time. Girls spend more than £13 a week while boys spend just over £11 a week.

Where does your money go?
✳ Two thirds of your money is spent on sweets and chocolates.
✳ Girls spend the rest on clothes, shoes, magazines and makeup.
✳ Boys spend the rest on more food and drink, computer games, DVDs and CDs.

Your choice

Tick the things you most like to spend money on:
✳ cinema/concert trips
✳ clothes
✳ sweets and snacks
✳ shoes, including trainers
✳ computer games
✳ sporting events
✳ books
✳ mobile phone and cards
✳ magazines
✳ cosmetics and toiletries
✳ CDs, DVDs
✳ other

Are you budgeting for all this?

You see some expensive trainers. Do you:
✳ save until you can buy them?
✳ earn money from chores?
✳ pester your parents for the extra cash?
✳ ask for them as an advance birthday gift?

Can you learn from your answers?

GIVE IT AWAY!

There are many, many people on our planet who need help. If you watch television news reports, or even see appeals in newspapers, you must be aware of how difficult life is for people in poor countries or war-torn places. If you plan to care about what goes on in the world and the people who share it with you – to be a 'citizen of the planet' and not a passive potato – then it's time to take an interest.

Refugees have fled from war or disasters at home. They live in makeshift homes until they can return.

Children receive food parcels from an overseas aid organisation.

EVERY little helps!

We all have **needs** and **wants**. Needs are things that we can't do without – things like food, water, clothing, and so on. Wants are things that we THINK we can't do without – things like ice cream, video games and designer clothes. But of course we can do without some of these 'wants' so we can help others. When you see pictures of refugees and the horror they're living through, it's difficult to see what you can do to help.

But 'every little helps' really does work here.

Helping abroad

We hear news every day of terrible poverty and hunger in overseas countries. You can shrug this off as being someone else's problem – it's all too far away anyway. And anyway, why can't their governments help them?

But when a few people have a lot of money and most are begging for food, things certainly seem unbalanced. It IS possible to change things. We can each do a little, knowing that this will add up to a lot in the end.

Homeless

Many people, even in rich countries, live homeless. Contributing to charities that help the homeless, takes them off the street and gives them shelter.

A great feeling

Giving to others less well off than yourself is not about going around feeling superior and smug. It's about knowing that someone out there will eat today because of what you've done.

And that has to make you feel you've done something worthwhile.

Charities

A helping hand

Charities are organisations that give help in many different forms to those in need. There are many well-known charities you will have heard of – and maybe helped from time to time.

These have an excellent reputation for rushing to a disaster zone and bringing immediate relief, as well as working over the long-term to improve education and health wherever they are based.

Foundations

Foundations are also charities. These are set up by wealthy companies, individuals or families to support certain projects with cash. Community foundations can be established to use specific funds for charitable purposes. They don't pay tax on their income, so they get the full benefit of their (and your) money.

Raising money

There's a charity walk planned. You have to walk around your local park and some outlying woods in a sponsored event. For each kilometre that you walk, various friends and family will sponsor you to the tune of 10p a kilometre. You could walk as a group, as a whole family, or your class at school could get involved. If there are another 50 people doing the same as you ... that's big bucks!

How much you give is entirely up to you, of course. Settle on an amount you feel comfortable with, and remember that however small this is, by giving regularly, the donation starts to build into something really meaningful.

And don't forget that giving money is just one way of helping. You can give toys, books and clothes to these same charities – it all helps.

RICH AND POOR

Many people think that if they were richer, they'd be happier. Of course, people who have enough to be able to feed and clothe themselves and live a comfortable life are far happier than those who don't. But once you are comfortable, does having more money bring more happiness? Well, being rich doesn't guarantee happiness, and being rich isn't the ONLY way to be happy.

The Struggle for Wealth

The great Indian leader Mohandas Gandhi believed that happiness came from living a simple life. Like many who follow the meaning of true religion, he rejected wealth as a means to fulfilment, even to the point of sewing his own clothing.

People who think wealth and happiness go together can find themselves on an upward slope – always struggling to be richer and richer, and becoming more and more unhappy because they can't make it. In the end, they feel as if they've failed – they never quite made it to the top. However, feeling content with what you've achieved is almost certainly the key to happiness.

Having it all

The amount of income a person earns, helps decide how much they buy. If a person with a low income spends £1,000 on a trip around the world, they will have to cut back on buying food, clothing or shelter. If a wealthy person makes the same investment, they may not need to cut anything.

When people earn more, they spend more – mostly on what are called normal goods, things like food, holidays and entertainment. They also cut back on what are called inferior goods. Public transport is an example – people stop taking the bus and start to drive their own cars.

Philanthropy

The rich don't just spend on themselves. Many give millions away to charities or other causes they support. Such people are known as philanthropists. Philanthropy means helping others.

Virtual money

In the future, you may completely lose coins and paper money as you see it today. Instead, you'll use plastic cards such as credit or debit cards for all transactions. In other words, money will go electronic. Or it may go even further. It may 'vanish' altogether!

So how can money be money when it doesn't look like money? In fact, when it doesn't look like anything because you can't even see it? You certainly can't pick it up and pop it in your purse.

Electronic money is money that passes from bank to bank, person to person, controlled by computers. The computers simply switch it from place to place using special codes.

AND THIS KIND OF MONEY DOESN'T HAVE TO BE REAL. IT CAN BE VIRTUAL.

Real or unreal?

This kind of money is called virtual currency or virtual money. 'Virtual' describes something that doesn't physically exist so that you can see or touch it, but computer software makes it seem so. It's very close to actually being something without actually being it.

Does this sound like the kind of money you would trust? Probably not – but virtual money operates like real money, and more and more people are starting to use it. Just like traditional money, these currencies can be used to buy physical goods and services.

Bitcoins

One of these kinds of currency, which is becoming popular, is the bitcoin. Bitcoins are electronically created and stored. Your piggy bank of bitcoins is in fact your computer. Bitcoins are exchanged using secret messaging for security so they can't be copied or stolen. And they don't belong to a bank or other institution so no one can interfere or control them.

Each bitcoin carries a code so if you use it to buy something there is a record of the deal. You can't use that bitcoin to buy something else – just like real money. If you spend it – it's gone!

For the future ...

In your own lifetime, you might just see the end of those jingling coins and paper notes. Technology is now learning to cope with the huge money transactions that speed round our planet on a minute by minute basis. There are likely to be more changes to the look and feel of money in the next 10 years than in the past 6000!

Round and Round

Today, huge amounts of money are shifted around the world in this way. Tomorrow, we may all deal in electronic money. You may accumulate THOUSANDS in your lifetime, but you'll never actually see a penny of it.

Money's money

All this probably won't affect you a great deal – unless you end up working in some kind of financial company. But you'll still have to earn money and pay the bills. The older you get, the more money will flow round and round you, bringing new responsibilities with it.

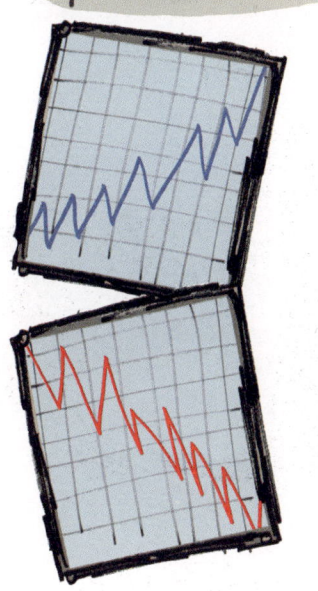

So the more you know about money, the better you'll be able to deal with it.

And the more you understand it...

... the more control over your money you'll have.

Let's discuss

Does money grow on trees?

Almost everybody wishes it did. Life might be a lot simpler. And we would have a lot more forests on the planet!

Unfortunately, money has a value and is exchanged for goods and services that also have a value. And it's precious stuff! Every penny you spend has to be earned – usually by your parents for each hour they work at their job.

How do you earn money?

If you're lucky, you'll be given an allowance to spend as you like. However, many parents believe that this pocket money should be earned. You can do this by helping around the house or running errands. What jobs could you do which would help your family? You can also ask neighbours or family friends if they will pay you to do some chores.

What's wrong with shopping?

Nothing at all if you really need to buy something. But DON'T shop for entertainment! Remember: the family budget is divided into necessities and luxuries so you need to spend sensibly. The best way is to write a list and stick to it. Think of some other ways you can control spending.

Why do you need a bank?

A bank account is essential for your parents so they can put their money somewhere safe and also pay the bills. You might have a piggy bank where you keep your allowance and any spare coins – but you can also save money in the bank.

If you put a little money in a savings account each week or month, the bank rewards you by paying you interest. Discuss how you can open a bank account and what you'd like to buy with your savings.

Why do you need to budget?

You will soon discover that money doesn't stretch to giving you everything you want. Those expensive items may just be out of reach. But savings do mount up, and if you know WHY you're saving – and WHAT the rewards will be – you'll get there faster.

Why not create a wish list with the price of each item so you know how much you need to save in your account? You could even give yourself a deadline to earn and save the money before a certain date.

Glossary

allowance
– see pocket money.
annum
Another word for year.
bank account
A person's agreement with a bank to look after their money.
bitcoin
An experimental currency which exists only in computer and internet buying and selling.
budget
An agreed sum to be spent.
charity
An organisation that gives help in many different forms to those in need.
consumer
A person who buys products on a regular basis and whose buying habits can be predicted.
credit
Money that is borrowed.
credit card
A card that lets you use borrowed money to buy goods.

currency
A form of money in notes and coins that is used for buying and selling.
debit
An amount taken out of a bank account as a payment.
debt
Borrowed money to be repaid.
depreciation
The value of something that gets lower over time.
donation
A gift of money, usually to a charity.
electronic money
Money that is not 'real' but which exists only in the world of internet and computers.
income
Money that is earned by working.
interest
A percentage sum added to borrowed or invested money.
loan
An amount of money that is given to someone but which must be paid back.

money cycle
Another word to describe how money moves round and round as it is used to buy and sell goods.

net worth
The total value of someone's personal money and valuable goods.

peer pressure
The phrase used to describe how people of the same age can influence each other to do things.

pester power
A phrase to describe how children can influence their parents to buy them things.

pocket money
Money paid to a child for their personal spending.

point of purchase
A special place in a shop where goods are displayed in an eye-catching way.

price
The cost of buying something.

profit
The money that is made by a seller which is more than the actual cost of the goods.

shopaholic
Someone who shops a lot and who needs to shop to feel happy.

spending power
A term used to describe the money available to spend of a particular group of people.

statistics
Mathematical figures that can be used to count how people behave.

virtual money
Money that exists in computer form only but which has an accepted value just like real money.

warranty
A guarantee that is issued by a seller when they sell products and which promises the products are in good condition and will be repaired if they are faulty.

Index

account 6, 10, 11, 20, 24, 25, 27, 55, 59, 60, 62
advertisement 28, 34, 36, 37, 46, 62
allowance 12, 13, 14, 16, 46, 58, 59, 60, 62
ATM (Automated Teller Machine) 24
bank 4, 6, 8, 9, 10, 11, 12, 19, 20, 21, 22, 23, 24, 25, 27, 42, 55, 59, 60, 62
bank account 6, 11, 24, 25, 55, 59, 60, 62
banknote 4
bankrupt 34
bargain. 34
bitcoin 55
borrowing 29, 40, 41, 42, 43
budget 3, 12, 40, 44, 45, 58, 59, 60, 62
charity 19, 35, 49, 50, 51, 53
charity shop 35
clearance stock 34
coin 4, 6, 8, 19, 54, 55, 59
compound interest 27
consumer 9, 36, 39
contract 14, 15
convenience store 31
credit 4, 42, 43, 45, 55, 60, 62
credit card 4, 42, 45, 60, 62
currency 4
current account 25
debit 4, 24, 55
debt 2, 40, 41, 42, 43, 60, 62
debt collector 42
deposit 24, 25
depreciate 26
donation 51
earning 6, 17
electronic money 4, 55
foundation 50
gold 4
goods 8, 26, 30, 32, 33, 38, 53, 58, 60
grant 6
happiness 3, 52
homelessness 49
income 12, 50, 53, 60, 61, 62
inherit 11
interest 19, 20, 24, 25, 27, 40, 41, 43, 48, 59, 60, 62, 63
internet 25, 62
invest 7, 9, 22, 24, 34
investments 25, 27
job 9, 15, 16, 58, 62
legal age 24
lending 27, 40, 55
loan 11, 40, 41, 63
money cycle 9
money management 9

net worth 11
note 4, 6, 54
online account 25
outlet stores 35
overseas aid 48
peer pressure 37
pester power 17
philanthropy 53
piggy bank 6, 19, 20, 22, 24, 59
pocket money 6, 13, 14, 16, 21, 42, 47, 58, 60, 63
point of purchase 33
post office 20
poverty 49, 60, 63
price 26, 31
product 31, 32, 33, 34, 35
profit 20, 27
pygg 23
ration book 38
refugee 48
refund 35
repayment 41, 43

sale 34
saving 4, 6, 10, 11, 18, 20, 21, 22, 24, 25, 27, 44, 59
savings account 10
savings bonds 11
shop 2, 8, 31, 32, 33, 34, 35, 38, 58, 63
shopaholic 39
shopping 28, 31, 32, 33, 35, 58
shop 30
simple interest 27, 63
spending 2, 3, 6 7, 9, 12, 13, 17, 18, 19, 20, 21, 26, 28, 29, 30, 31, 33, 34, 36, 37, 43, 44, 46, 47, 53, 58
spending power 36, 46
statement 25, 60
statistics 3, 46
stock 31, 34, 35
store 31, 32, 33, 35
street vendor 34

tax 50, 60, 61, 62, 63
trust money 11
tween 46
value 5, 13, 20, 26, 28, 58
virtual money 55
warranty 34
wealth 3, 52
will 11
work 6, 9, 14, 16, 22, 31, 48, 58, 60, 61, 63

绿色印刷　保护环境　爱护健康

亲爱的读者朋友：

　　本书已入选"北京市绿色印刷工程——优秀出版物绿色印刷示范项目"。它采用绿色印刷标准印制，在封底印有"绿色印刷产品"标志。

　　按照国家环境标准（HJ2503-2011）《环境标志产品技术要求 印刷 第一部分：平版印刷》，本书选用环保型纸张、油墨、胶水等原辅材料，生产过程注重节能减排，印刷产品符合人体健康要求。

　　选择绿色印刷图书，畅享环保健康阅读！

北京市绿色印刷工程

图书在版编目（CIP）数据

个人理财：你是如何花钱的？为什么要花钱？：汉、英／（英）贝利，（英）劳著；（英）比奇插图；傅瑞蓉 译．—北京：华夏出版社，2016.1

（华夏少儿金融智慧屋．货币系列）

书名原文：Your Money：How You Spend Your Money，and Why？

ISBN 978-7-5080-8703-0

Ⅰ.①个… Ⅱ.①贝… ②劳… ③比… ④傅… Ⅲ.①私人投资—少儿读物—汉、英 Ⅳ.①F830.59-49

中国版本图书馆CIP数据核字（2015）第306743号

Your Money: How You Spend Your Money,and Why?
Copyright © 2014 BrambleKids Ltd
All rights reserved
The simplified Chinese translation rights arranged through Rightol Media（本书中文简体版权经由锐拓传媒取得Email:copyright@rightol.com）
CHINESE SIMPLIFIED Language adaptation edition published by BrambleKids Ltd., and HUAXIA PUBLISHING HOUSE Copyright © 2016
All Rights Reserved
版权所有　翻版必究
北京市版权局著作权合同登记号：图字 01-2015-2439

个人理财——你是如何花钱的？为什么要花钱？

作　者	［英］格里·贝利　　［英］费利西娅·劳
插　图	［英］马克·比奇
译　者	傅瑞蓉
责任编辑	李雪飞

出版发行	华夏出版社
经　销	新华书店
印　装	北京中科印刷有限公司
版　次	2016年1月北京第1版　2016年1月北京第1次印刷
开　本	787×1030　1/16
印　张	8
字　数	140千字
定　价	39.80元

华夏出版社　地址：北京市东直门外香河园北里4号　邮编：100028
网址：www.hxph.com.cn　电话：（010）64663331（转）
若发现本版图书有印装质量问题，请与我社营销中心联系调换。